Faculty–Librarian Relationships

CHANDOS
INFORMATION PROFESSIONAL SERIES

Series Editor: Ruth Rikowski
(email: rikowski@tiscali.co.uk)

Chandos' new series of books are aimed at the busy information professional. They have been specially commissioned to provide the reader with an authoritative view of current thinking. They are designed to provide easy-to-read and (most importantly) practical coverage of topics that are of interest to librarians and other information professionals. If you would like a full listing of current and forthcoming titles, please visit our web site **www.chandospublishing.com** or contact Hannah Grace-Williams on email info@chandospublishing.com or telephone number +44 (0) 1865 884447.

New authors: we are always pleased to receive ideas for new titles; if you would like to write a book for Chandos, please contact Dr Glyn Jones on email gjones@chandospublishing.com or telephone number +44 (0)1865 884447.

Bulk orders: some organisations buy a number of copies of our books. If you are interested in doing this, we would be pleased to discuss a discount. Please contact Hannah Grace-Williams on email info@chandospublishing.com or telephone number +44 (0) 1865 884447.

Faculty–Librarian Relationships

PAUL O. JENKINS

Chandos Publishing
Oxford • England

Chandos Publishing (Oxford) Limited
Chandos House
5 & 6 Steadys Lane
Stanton Harcourt
Oxford OX29 5RL
UK
Tel: +44 (0) 1865 884447 Fax: +44 (0) 1865 884448
Email: info@chandospublishing.com
www.chandospublishing.com

First published in Great Britain in 2005

ISBN:
1 84334 116 6 (paperback)
1 84334 117 4 (hardback)

© Paul O. Jenkins, 2005

British Library Cataloguing-in-Publication Data.
A catalogue record for this book is available from the British Library.

Cover images courtesy of Bytec Solutions Ltd (*www.bytecweb.com*) and David Hibberd (*DAHibberd@aol.com*).

Printed in the UK and USA.

To Emily, Owen, and Thomas Owen

Contents

Acknowledgements

A hearty thanks to all the wonderful librarians I've had the pleasure to work with during my tenure in the profession and who have taught me so much: Cheryl Albrecht, Mark Cain, Anne Chase, Susan Falgner, Susan DiRenzo, Christina Diefenbach, Daphne Miller, Beth Rile, Julie Flanders, Jim Layden, Cynthia Gregory, Karen Berger (née Stockland), Tim Browning, Jim Krailler, David Hodgins, Karen Peppers, Carolmarie Stock, Eileen Wedig, Char Gildea, Jackie and Jason Buydos, Mary Ruebusch, Sr. Elizabeth Brown, Janet Lake, Marie Murphy, and Carole Allgyer.

The faculty of the College of Mount St. Joseph have been and continue to be a pleasure to serve. Special thanks to those who contributed to this book: Alan de Courcy, John Trokan, Sr. Annette Muckerheide, Dan Mader, Elizabeth 'Buffy' Barkley, Jack Hettinger, Jeff Hillard, Jim Bodle, Mary Kay Jordan Fleming, Mike Klabunde, Sr. Peg McPeak, Richard Sparks, Ron White, Shirley Hoenigman, Sue Johnson, and Tim Lynch. Tom Seibert and Bill Schutzius served as excellent mentors, and I am grateful for the friendship of Gene Kritsky, Jerry Bellas, Jim Green, Sharon Kesterson Bollen, Loyola Walter, Meg Riestenberg, Darla Vale, and Suzanne Schindler.

I am indebted to the following librarians who helped me revise the manuscript of this book: Larry Hardesty, Julie Deardorff, Mark Cain, Mary Ledoux, and Michelle Sarff.

Larry Hardesty was kind enough to write the foreword to this book. Larry has long been an inspiration to me and many others in the profession.

My brothers Hugh and Clay, my sister Carol, and my mother continue to serve as intellectual benchmarks.

Finally, I thank Dr. Glyn Jones and Chandos for their faith in me.

Foreword

I first met Paul Jenkins almost ten years ago when he first became the director of Library Services at the College of Mount Saint Joseph and participated in the College Library Directors' Mentor Program. Even in his first year as a young college library director, Paul exhibited an extraordinary understanding of the ways of the college classroom faculty.

Paul grew up in a faculty family and his experiences during his formative years helped to mold his attitudes toward classroom faculty. This background, combined with Paul's evenhanded personality and keen intellect, fostered his perceptive insights into the nuances and complexities of classroom faculty culture and allowed him to offer them in this work. He does so with candor but also with optimism and without invoking negative stereotypes.

Understanding classroom faculty is, of course, of considerable importance. As noted by Bowen and Schuster almost twenty years ago:

> The nation's faculties are entrusted with the education for about a third to a half of every cohort of young people, and they touch the lives of millions of other persons in less intensive counters. They train virtually the entire leadership of society in the professions, government, business, and to a lesser extent, the arts. Especially, they train the teachers, clergy, journalists, physicians, and others whose main function is the informing, shaping, and guiding of human development. (Bowen and Schuster, 1986: 3)

Yet, despite the role faculty members play in the education of students, and, in particular, for our purposes here, the use of the academic library, there is a long history of observers (both librarians and others) who have concluded that classroom faculty members have not fully engaged students in the use of the academic library.

As early as 1940, in his seminal work, *Teaching with Books*, Harvie Branscomb concluded, 'Books bought by the library lie unused on the shelves because instructors in large numbers are not depending upon volumes to supply any essential elements in the education process for which they are responsible' (Branscomb, 1940: 79). Almost twenty years later, another luminary in academic library history, Patricia Knapp, re-inforced this perspective in writing, 'Where the instructor expected and planned for student use of the library, it occurred. Where he did not, it did not occur' (Knapp, 1958: 829). In the early 1960s, the eminent Guy Lyle lamented, 'Present teaching practices would appear to provide little incentive for students to do substantial and rewarding reading. If pro-fessors are wedded to the idea of using textbooks and reserve materials, there is little the librarian can do about making changes' (Lyle, 1963: 56).

As a result, relationships between classroom faculty members and li-brarians are often depicted as adversarial and antagonistic. There is supposedly something incongruent between the values and beliefs of the classroom faculty members and those of the academic librarians. Some observers believe that the predominant culture of classroom faculty im-pedes further integration into the curriculum of undergraduate use of the library. For example, librarian Knapp described her strategies for in-creasing student use of the library as 'Bucking the System' (Knapp, 1971: 217). Robert Blackburn, a professor of higher education, wrote about the tensions between the two groups (Blackburn, 1968). Maurice P. March-ant and Mary Biggs, writing more than a decade apart, elaborated further from the perspective of librarians about the 'eternal conflicts' between classroom faculty members and librarians (Marchant, 1968; Biggs, 1981).

Paul, however, rejects the notion that librarians and classroom faculty are natural antagonists. In this book he displays an understanding of the character of the classroom faculty, how their values and attitudes are shaped, and the pressures they are under. These values, attitudes, and pressures are further illuminated through the interviews Paul did with College of Mount St. Joseph faculty. Paul comprehends that successful collaboration with the classroom faculty for the benefit of students does not come from confrontations but through the earning of trust and colleagueship. While typically librarians may well be at a disadvantage in academia because they do not possess the PhD and the research skills and subject specialization that go with it, Paul demonstrates how librarians can gain respect from classroom faculty members. Classroom faculty members respect intellectual ability, evenhandedness, and an appreciation for scholarship. They respect someone who displays a genuine interest in their work and the work of their students.

These are salient considerations for the reader to keep in mind in reading how one librarian at a small college successfully joins in partnership with the classroom faculty at that institution. Paul puts into plain words how a willingness to collaborate with faculty members and to share in their passions and enthusiasm accomplishes much more than complaints and confrontations. A simple gesture, such as soliciting a list of recommended books from classroom faculty members, can accomplish substantial inroads in establishing positive relationships. Keeping these points in mind will help the reader to understand Paul's success and how the reader can use this information in working with the classroom faculty members at his/her institution. This is a valuable book that handles a challenging topic with tact and diplomacy. It is a must read for anyone considering becoming or anyone who already is an academic librarian.

Dr. Larry Hardesty
University of Nebraska at Kearney

Note

Dr. Larry Hardesty is Dean of the Library at the University of Nebraska at Kearney and is the author of, among other publications, *Faculty and the Library: The Undergraduate Experience*, Ablex Press, 1991, and 'Faculty culture and bibliographic instruction: an exploratory analysis,' *Library Trends*, 44 (Fall 1995): 339–67.

References

Biggs, M. (1981) 'Sources of tensions and conflict between librarians and faculty', *Journal of Higher Education*, 52: 182–201.

Blackburn, R.T. (1968) 'College libraries – indicated failures: some reasons – and a possible remedy,' *College and Research Libraries*, 29: 171–7.

Bowen, H.R. and Schuster, J.H. (1986) *American Professors: A National Resource Imperiled*. New York: Oxford University Press.

Branscomb, H. (1940) *Teaching With Books*. Chicago: Association of American Colleges, American Library Association.

Knapp, P. (1958) 'College teaching and the library,' *Illinois Libraries*, 40: 828–33.

Knapp, P. (1971) 'Guidelines for bucking the system: a strategy for moving towards the ideal of the undergraduate library as a teaching instrument,' *Drexel Library Quarterly*, 7: 217–21.

Lyle, G.R. (1963) *The President, the Professor, and the College Library.* New York: H.W. Wilson.

Marchant, M.P. (1969) 'Faculty–library conflict,' *Library Journal*, 94: 2886–9.

Introduction

The context of my experiences with faculty

'A wise son maketh a glad father.' *Proverbs*

For forty-five years, my father was a Professor of English Literature at Carleton College (Northfield, Minnesota), a small (1,900 students) highly selective, private, liberal arts undergraduate institution. As I grew up, I was thus privy to many dinner-time conversations detailing the activities of his colleagues. Many drew his gentle scorn; fewer his praise. Mysterious terms like 'tenure' and 'sabbatical' filled the air. Frequent references to someone known only as 'the Dean' were made. I quickly gained the impression that the life of the college professor was somehow different from other, more mundane careers. Occasionally at my parents' dinner parties I would encounter the faces behind the names. I remember being surprised at how charming they all were.

I took great pride in being a 'faculty brat'. I was certain to include the fact in conversations with new acquaintances. That my father was a man of great learning somehow seemed to raise my status too. I spent many hours at the Carleton Library, pouring over Art History books, hoping that exposure to all these great books would further heighten my lofty status. Spending time in the stacks struck me as a great privilege, an opportunity to separate myself from the everyday existence most others endured.

Still, I never imagined that I might one day teach at the college level. My father, in fact, counseled me and my siblings against it. Though he didn't go into great detail, I sensed that he wanted us to do something more valuable with our lives. Perhaps the years of petty squabbling so typical – I would learn – of campus politics had taken their toll. In contrast to his own very verbal profession, he admired those who created something more significant with their skills.

During my undergraduate days at Lawrence University, a small, private liberal arts college in Wisconsin, I met many professors who seemed familiar. Thanks to my father, they had lived in my mind for years as types. Reluctant as I was to fall prey to overgeneralization, I couldn't help but pigeonhole a few as typical of their kind. I met the researcher who was more concerned with his work out of the classroom than inside it; the devoted teacher who just wanted to teach and had no desire to add more grist to the already overflowing academic mill; the challenger who delighted in startling his charges and asking them to examine their own lives and confront their own fears; the entertainer whose classroom was his stage; the long-tenured relic, holding on as best he could until retirement. Happily, however, the majority of faculty I met as an undergraduate defied such crude classification. They were bright, eager, and curious men and women, devoted to their students and their profession, both good scholars and good teachers, and cynical only when circumstances presented them with no other choice.

When I decided to enter graduate school in library science, my father the professor was delighted. He had always held librarians in high esteem as the stewards of knowledge. Unlike too many others on campus, he continued, librarians avoided the sloughs of politics and simply did their job. They were uniformly helpful, responsible, and agreeable. I think he believed that the printed word was better able to educate students than many of his colleagues. Meanwhile, my older brother had chosen to follow in our father's footsteps. He had entered a graduate program in English at a revered Ivy League institution. Some years later my younger sister trumped my bachelor's degree in German and pursued a doctoral degree in the same field in St. Louis. My oldest brother was already a lawyer, so by the time I earned my Master's in Library Science (MLS) I felt I occupied the lower end of the family totem poll.

It's worth mentioning that as the youngest of three brothers I became used to the concept of serving others quite early in life. This role came naturally to me and I don't recall ever regarding it as a burden. I respected my brothers and wanted to please them. They didn't take advantage of my willingness (at least not very often) and acknowledged what I would today call my good service orientation. I include this detail because serving campus faculty became an extension of an ethic that had long existed in me.

In graduate school I took an elective course named simply 'Academic Librarianship.' I'd already completed a number of required courses and was pretty certain I was going to seek work at a college or university. Our instructor continually stressed the importance of nurturing good relationships with campus faculty. As an aside, he also mentioned that they could be hard to work with at times. I noticed my peers scratching down this note, but I didn't need to. I flattered myself that I already knew what professors were like.

In 1988, fresh out of graduate school, I was hired as the Head of Collection Development by the College of Mount St. Joseph (Cincinnati, OH). Like Carleton College and Lawrence University, the Mount, as it is affectionately known, is a small, private liberal arts institution. There, I soon discovered, the similarities end. Carleton and Lawrence are very rich compared to the Mount. Their endowments, $451 million and $164 million, respectively, dwarf the Mount's $16 million endowment. Their libraries hold 662,000 and 376,000 volumes compared to the Mount's 100,000. Eighty-nine per cent of Carleton's 220 faculty members are full-time and 91 per cent hold the terminal degree. At Lawrence, 78 per cent of the 166 faculty members are full-time, and 79 per cent hold the terminal degree. Only 60 per cent of the faculty at the Mount are full-time and of these, only 49 per cent hold the terminal degree.

Upon my arrival at the Mount, I remember thinking, 'where's the rest of the library?' I was still clinging to the notion that a library's worth is measured by the size of its collection. Nevertheless, I will also admit to feeling intimidated when I reported for work on my first day. Before entering graduate school I had never worked an hour in any library. I was a seasoned library user, but what kind of librarian would I make? I had been around college professors nearly my whole life, but I had yet to work with one as a colleague. How could I get to know them better, I wondered? More importantly, how could they get to know me? As I sat in my office, I remembered seeing a list of recommended books which college professors from some famous institution had compiled for their students. Their selections varied greatly and reflected their particular interests. Surely soliciting such a list from Mount faculty would be an effective way for us to become better acquainted.

My library director approved the project and I contacted the faculty after the initial crush of the fall semester had subsided. I asked them to list five books they thought a Mount graduate should have read by the time he graduates. Nearly half of the faculty responded with their suggestions. This information served as a first bridge I could use to learn more about their personal interests. I learned, for example, that Dr. Kritsky had a passion for Charles Darwin; that Dr. Aber had social concerns, listing authors like John Steinbeck, Paulo Freire, and Michael Harrington; that Art Professor Sharon Kesterson Bollen favored the classics – Homer, Dante, Cervantes, Shakespeare; that Jeff Hillard, our poet in residence, loved the novels of Gabriel Garcia Marquez. Once compiled and disseminated, the list sparked a campus-wide discussion on great books and the established canons of literature.

As an introduction to the list and its purposes, I included my choices along with a brief rationale:

> Whether by subconscious design, or merely by happy accident, my choices treat five themes which must concern every young mind: faith, art, intellect, race, and our relationship with our parents. I, the bookworm, read *Robinson Crusoe* seeking only diversion. What I found, however, was a moving portrait of one man's emerging (or reemerging) faith. I, the student, read *The Great Gatsby* for the first time because it was assigned to me. After two subsequent voluntary readings, I remained astonished by Fitzgerald's artistry. I, the rather ashamed German major, read *The Magic Mountain* only after I had received my B.A. in German. Never have I worked so hard to climb any mountain; never have I appreciated one man's intellect as much as I do Thomas Mann's. I, the American, read *Uncle Tom's Cabin* wondering what all the fuss was about, and wondering at the ability of the printed word to help change history. More than any news footage of the march to Washington, more than stories of turmoil in the South reported on the evening news, this work of fiction finally made me confront the issue of race in America. Finally, I, the lover of Russian literature, bathed in the words of Ivan Turgenev's *Fathers and Sons*. I viewed the novel both as a time capsule of sorts, and as a living – and sometimes distressing – reminder that the more things change, the more they stay the same. That is, in some ways fathers and sons will never understand the concerns of the other's generation.

The list proved an effective ice-breaker. The months that followed were full of continued communication with faculty, both formal and informal. I discovered that accidental meetings near faculty mail boxes (which I was stuffing with book reviews) and conversations in the cafeteria yielded as many concrete results as did those scheduled and held in our offices. Now that I had identified authors and areas of particular interest I opened an unrelenting campaign of selective dissemination of information (SDI) with my faculty. The number of book requests picked up substantially, and I began to feel more confident in making my own selections. I was informed by other members of the library staff that professors who had long ago 'given up' on the library were returning – and with them their students.

Another list further cemented my relationship to the faculty. Designed as both a morale raiser, and a way to show the administration and the Board of Trustees how much research was going on at the Mount, a teaching college, I solicited from faculty a list of their recent (past three years) publications and research interests. (This latter category was included so as not to disenfranchise those faculty who had not to date published a great deal.) Once more, the list helped acquaint me with faculty so that I might forward to them materials of interest. It also indicated to them that I was on their side. After all, who doesn't like to be presented with an opportunity to do a little bragging? The list has since been updated every three to five years.

In my third year of college service, as a member of the campus grievance committee, I became involved in a situation that would have great ramifications both for the faculty and for me personally. Serving on this committee cemented the bond of trust I had begun to establish with the faculty. My open participation in these meetings convinced the faculty that I was not only a librarian, but also a member of the college community committed to improving campus conditions. When a dispute arose between a fired faculty member (a department chair) and the administration, the committee sought out tenured faculty members who would be willing to serve as chair of an ad hoc hearing panel. More than a dozen faculty were recruited for the position, but none accepted. Needless to say, the campus became charged with fear, mistrust, and doubt. To quell the committee's frustration I offered to serve as hearing panel chair. I'm still not certain what prompted me to make this move. It was probably a combination of youthful bravado and simple naiveté. In any case, I was about to make a name for myself among the faculty. Many congratulated me on my courage; more questioned my sanity.

The hearing took three days. Besides me, the panel included single representatives from both the grievant and the administration. The three of us listened as lawyers for the two parties pled their case. To cut a long story short, we found in favor of the faculty member. Though she lost her position as chair, she was reinstated. Though it was drafted by the lawyer chosen by the College to advise the hearing panel, I signed my name to the 'Findings of Fact, Conclusions and Decisions' as instructed. Word of the decision spread quickly across campus and my status among faculty rose. Now, after having appeared many times before the assembled Faculty Council, after having 'stood up' to the administration, after having spent many hours outside the library as well as within it, I was a more familiar face than I had ever intended. I felt I had paid my dues and looked forward to a time of lessened responsibility.

That spring, however, I was nominated for election to the Executive Committee of Faculty Council (ECFC), the faculty governing body. While flattered, I didn't imagine that the faculty would choose me, a non-teacher, to serve such an important post. To my surprise I was elected; to my astonishment the other members of ECFC then asked me to serve as chair. I was to represent the interests of the faculty, set the agenda for Faculty Council meetings, speak for the faculty on Board of Trustees committees, and even carry the ceremonial mace at the head of the faculty procession at Commencement exercises. Still baby-faced at age of 29, I recall overhearing a member of the audience on that occasion comment on how nice it was that the College was letting a student lead the faculty procession.

Soon after, I began teaching courses at the Mount. In a fit of enthusiasm I had written a small pamphlet titled 'Dickens for the Uninitiated.' I'd first read *David Copperfield* as a teenager and by the third chapter I knew the author would be a life-long friend. The purpose of my self-published booklet was to clear up what I felt were some injustices that had been done to Dickens by the high-school teachers of America. By having their students read *Hard Times*, or *A Tale of Two Cities* (his two shortest novels), these teachers had left their students with the impression that Dickens's world was one of unremitting gloom. My short essay was designed to reintroduce to the uninitiated the fact that Dickens remains English literature's greatest comic novelist; that largely forgotten novels like *The Pickwick Papers* and *Martin Chuzzlewit* abounded in humor. When I had finished I had no idea what to do with the paper. As an afterthought I forwarded a copy to Tom Seibert, a distinguished member of the English department. My thought was that he might have an occasion to give a copy to a promising student who appreciated literature but was ignorant of Dickens's gift for language and humor.

A few weeks later, Professor Seibert surprised and delighted me by asking if I would be interested in teaching an auto-study course on my favorite author. The auto-study courses at the Mount are designed to give students an opportunity to study areas of interest that are not usually offered as a classroom experience. While a Dickens novel was always included in the regularly offered Nineteenth-Century English

Novel course, this auto-study would give students a chance to explore the author in much greater depth. Like independent study courses, auto-studies had no regularly scheduled class time. The student and instructor meet as necessary. After reminding Mr. Seibert that my qualifications to teach the course were simply a good understanding of how to study literature (my undergraduate degree was in German literature) and a mania for Dickens, he assured me that reading my pamphlet had convinced him that I was qualified. Members of the English department began regularly recommending my course to their advisees. Over the next ten years I tried to show more than twenty students – one at a time – that Dickens wrote for the common man and, while he was eager to acquaint him with nineteenth-century England's ills, he also wanted to make him laugh.

Having heard good things about my auto-study from one of his students, another member of the English department, Jack Hettinger, gave me the opportunity to team-teach *David Copperfield* in his Nineteenth-Century English Novel course. In their course evaluations, several students noted my participation as one of the highlights of the class. Jack thanked me in writing for my participation. 'Your wisdom and methods,' he wrote, 'benefited the students and me greatly. The discussion you inspired and sustained was equally rewarding. I want to single out one benefit of your instruction. I'm pleased that the students had an opportunity to see another teacher model with skill and felicity some different approaches than mine. Until you joined us, I simply hadn't been able to treat in depth as many critical maneuvers as I had wished. You performed yeoman service on this score.' Later, I was made an honorary member of the Humanities department.

A third mentor, my library director, Mark Cain, had inspired me to begin participating more actively in the profession, including attending national conferences and seeking publishing opportunities. His enthusiasm for academic librarianship lit a fire under me. Until his arrival I had concentrated on local duties for the College. Under his tutelage I expanded my horizons beyond the seven hills of Cincinnati. I achieved modest success with three short articles on collection development, and understood for the first time that library conferences were not a waste of time but rather occasions to learn from others who are more experienced in the field.

In my eighth year at the College, with teaching experience under my belt, three publications to my name, and having served the highest campus committee office available, I felt ready to pursue promotion.

I made some inquiries and confirmed what I had suspected: no other librarian had ever applied for promotion. Librarians were assigned the rank of instructor upon beginning their duties and three years later were automatically promoted to Assistant Professor, with no increase in salary. To gain promotion to Associate Professor (and add $2,000 to my salary) I would have to apply in the same manner as any other faculty member. I assembled a bulky portfolio to state my case. In addition to self-evaluations on professional competence, scholarship, and academic citizenship, my immediate supervisor, three peer evaluators, and three external evaluators of my choosing rated my progress in these three areas. The biggest problem, of course, was how to evaluate my teaching, the major component of a faculty evaluation. Most of my instructional skills were displayed in informal encounters at the Reference Desk and generalized bibliographic instruction sessions. My experiences in the classroom, while more frequent than others in my position, were, nevertheless, minimal.

Shortly before Christmas I was informed that I had been promoted. Almost with his next breath, however, my boss told me that the promotion procedures for librarians needed to be revised. The committee hadn't been sure how to handle my application since it was the first of its kind. Since our responsibilities did differ markedly from our teaching colleagues, we should be evaluated on a different set of criteria. The following semester, my supervisor, the Academic Dean, and I created a new set of guidelines for the evaluation of librarians. While details were numerous, in essence we separated ourselves from the faculty by changing our designations from Instructor, Assistant, Associate, and (full) Professor to a numerical system often employed in Public Library hierarchies. New professionals entering the workforce would be called Librarian I, those with more than three years of experience would be called Librarian II. Promotion from I to II would be based on a one-year trial period, and the Library Director alone would make the decision. Those seeking promotion from II to III would submit a packet to the Library Director, Academic Dean, and Chief Information Officer (following an increasingly typical model, the library at the Mount reports to the CIO instead of to the Dean). Unlike its equivalent for teaching faculty, the packet for librarian-faculty would place more emphasis on professional development and service excellence, and less on teaching and scholarship.

My first status-conscious reaction to the new guidelines was to lament my sudden transformation from the rather lofty perch of Associate

Professor to the drab designation of Librarian III. I had reveled in the fact that, even without a PhD, I was regarded by many of the teaching faculty as a true peer. After all, I had been promoted under their guidelines. My more pragmatic side recognized that for the vast majority of current and future librarians at the Mount, separating ourselves from teaching faculty was appropriate and palatable. Our basic privileges – serving on faculty committees and being eligible for promotion and raises – remained. Even under the old system, we had not been eligible for tenure, so we had really lost only the prestige that emanates from the designations of academic nomenclature.

So today I write as a Librarian III, not as an Associate Professor. Yet my experiences with the teaching faculty at the Mount have made me feel their equal, their active partner in the education of our students. It is with a reinforced knowledge of these faculty partners that I offer the following chapters so that future academic librarians might enter the game with a better understanding of its players. While my experiences have been limited to a single campus, I am confident that many of the issues I discuss and recommendations I make are applicable to all academic libraries.

My interviews with College of Mount St. Joseph faculty constitute an important part of this book and make up its fifth chapter. An excellent way for readers to begin to cultivate their understanding of the faculty psyche is to read these interviews in their entirety. I have used **bold font** to identify Mount St. Joseph faculty quoted within the text of the first four chapters. Occasionally, when the subject matter is sensitive, I have listed them as anonymous.

Finally, while I realize that females outnumber males in the world of librarianship, I find myself unable to forsake the convention I learned as the son of an English professor to use masculine pronouns to refer to an indefinite person. I trust that my female readers will forgive me.

About the author

Paul O. Jenkins grew up in the college town of Northfield, Minnesota, the son of an English professor. Inspired by his parents, his siblings, and their enormous book collection, he soon became an avid reader. After graduating with a degree in German Literature from Lawrence University (Appleton, Wisconsin) in 1983, he enrolled in the Library Science graduate program at the University of Wisconsin and received his MLS there in 1987. From 1988 to the present he has worked at the College of Mount St. Joseph (Cincinnati, OH), first as Head of Collection Development, then, beginning in 1995, as Director of Library Services. An active faculty member there, Jenkins has taught courses on the novels of Charles Dickens and the history of American protest music. In his spare time he enjoys soccer, tennis, painting military miniatures, and playing the harmonica and concertina. He resides in Cincinnati with his wife, Emily, and son, Tom.

The author may be contacted at:

paul_jenkins@mail.msj.edu

The faculty: who they are, how they think

'I am a teacher at heart, and there are moments in the classroom when I can hardly hold the joy... But at other moments, the classroom is so lifeless or painful or confused – and I am powerless to do anything about it – that my claim to be a teacher seems a transparent sham.' – Parker Palmer, from *The Courage to Teach*

In his seminal book, *Faculty and the Library: The Undergraduate Experience*, Larry Hardesty writes: 'While librarians are part of academia, they seldom either share or fully appreciate the values of the faculty' (Hardesty, 1991: 67). To really make a difference, he notes later, 'librarians need to understand the complexities of faculty culture' (32). Writing in 1981, Biggs described a relationship that needed to be improved.

> Librarians and faculty members were once creatures of the same order, with similar educational preparation, interests, and understanding of what the library should do. Rather quickly they have evolved into quite different creatures, each insistent upon professional autonomy, stubbornly holding sometimes disparate visions of the library's mission, and communicating very little with each other. (Biggs, 1981: 186)

While I don't believe that the two groups are still such antagonists, in order to improve our relationships with them, it is important that we examine our sometimes misunderstood partners in academe, the teaching faculty.

Demographics

Before exploring the less measurable aspects of the faculty psyche, let us examine some demographic data. Every year *The Chronicle of Higher Education* publishes its Almanac Issue. According to the 2004–2005 edition, there are more than 600,000 full-time faculty members in the United States who hold the rank of instructor or lecturer (20 per cent), assistant professor (26 per cent), associate professor (24 per cent), or professor (30 per cent). Another 500,000 faculty teach on a part-time basis. This group has grown from representing 34 per cent of faculty in 1979 to 44 per cent in the latest survey. The increased use of adjunct faculty has become a serious concern to many in academia. Of full-time faculty, 62 per cent are male, 81 per cent Caucasian. They enjoy high status in society. 'In the United States, only physicians outrank professors in occupational prestige. In the rest of the world, professors have the highest prestige rating of all occupations, physicians rating only second or lower' (Falk, 1990: 225). They are quite an exclusive bunch. Of all undergraduates, 1 in 7 goes on to pursue an MA, but only 1 in 50 a PhD (Wilson, 1995: 33). Fewer still complete their doctorate.

The Higher Education Research Institute (HERI) survey, conducted on a triennial basis, is a treasure trove of additional information. More than 32,000 full-time college and university faculty members in the United States completed the latest survey, conducted in 2001–2002. From the survey we learn that 8 per cent of faculty are younger than 35; 22 per cent are between the ages of 35 and 44; 35 per cent between 45 and 54; 30 per cent between 55 and 64; and 6 per cent are 65 or older. The most popular personal goals of faculty members were to raise a family (endorsed by 73 per cent), develop a meaningful philosophy of life (76 per cent), and to help others in difficulty (64 per cent). Seventy-seven per cent of faculty indicate that they are satisfied with their jobs, up from 75 per cent in 1998, and 69 per cent in 1989. Data for all respondents indicate that 59 per cent of faculty are interested in both teaching and research. Of the remaining 41 per cent, 37 per cent were interested 'very heavily in teaching,' while only 4 per cent were interested 'very heavily in research.' Why do faculty members choose their profession? 84 per cent cited the 'intellectual challenge'; 77 per cent its 'intellectual freedom'; 75 per cent 'freedom to pursue my scholarly/teaching interests'; and 73 per cent the job's autonomy (Lindholm, 2002).

Classification of colleges and universities

What kinds of institutions employ faculty? Originally established in 1973, the Carnegie Classification of Institutions of Higher Education is 'the leading typology of American colleges and universities' (available online at: *http://www.carnegiefoundation.org/Classification/*). Via this classification, the 'institutional diversity' of American higher education is defined. The latest (2000) update identifies eight major categories.

- *Doctoral/research universities – extensive*. These institutions typically offer a wide range of baccalaureate programs and they are committed to graduate education through the doctorate. During the period studied, they awarded 50 or more doctoral degrees per year across at least 15 disciplines.

- *Doctoral/research universities – intensive*. These institutions typically offer a wide range of baccalaureate programs and they are committed to graduate education through the doctorate. During the period studied, they awarded at least ten doctoral degrees per year across three or more disciplines, or at least 20 doctoral degrees per year overall.

- *Master's colleges and universities* (i). These institutions typically offer a wide range of baccalaureate programs and they are committed to graduate education through the master's degree. During the period studied, they awarded 40 or more master's degrees per year across three or more disciplines.

- *Master's colleges and universities* (ii). These institutions typically offer a wide range of baccalaureate programs and they are committed to graduate education through the master's degree. During the period studied, they awarded 20 or more master's degrees per year.

- *Baccalaureate colleges – liberal arts*. These institutions are primarily undergraduate colleges with major emphasis on baccalaureate programs. During the period studied, they awarded at least half of their baccalaureate degrees in liberal arts fields.

- *Baccalaureate colleges – general*. These institutions are primarily undergraduate colleges with major emphasis on baccalaureate programs. During the period studied, they awarded less than half of their baccalaureate degrees in liberal arts fields.

- *Baccalaureate/associate's colleges.* These institutions are undergraduate colleges where the majority of conferrals are below the baccalaureate level (associate's degrees and certificates). During the period studied, bachelor's degrees accounted for at least 10 per cent of undergraduate awards.

- *Associate's colleges.* These institutions offer associate's degree and certificate programs but, with few exceptions, award no baccalaureate degrees. This group includes institutions where, during the period studied, bachelor's degrees represented less than 10 per cent of all undergraduate awards.

Numerous specialized institutions are also defined, including theological seminaries, medical schools, and schools of engineering, business, art, or music. No corresponding definitions exist for European institutions.

Profile of faculty traits, concerns, and attitudes

Levine has identified the following characteristics of faculty. (1) They are very intelligent. Their IQ scores place them in the top 5–10 per cent of the population in the United States. (2) They have a sound general education. That is, they have the ability to communicate well, both verbally and with the pen. (3) They are by nature contemplative and possess keen intellectual curiosity. (4) They display open-mindedness and tolerance, something to be expected from a profession based largely on intellectual freedom. (5) They have mastered a specialized field. (6) They are self-motivated, both need and desire little direct supervision, and are often stubbornly independent (Levine, 1978: 176–8). Hazard Adams puts it more boldly. 'Eccentricity is a symbol of the scholar's intellectual freedom, to say nothing of his stubbornness' (Adams, 1988: 13).

It is this last characteristic that can make working with faculty difficult for librarians, or, for that matter, any other college staff. In graduate school, faculty have spent years in largely solitary research, honing their craft under the supervision of a selected few mentors. Hard-won doctorate in hand, they enter their classroom feeling a justifiable pride. There they are the absolute authority. While governed by campus and/or professional curricular guidelines, and remotely supervised by department chair and Academic Dean, they write their own syllabi, choose their own textbooks, and put their own personal spin on the topic at hand. Think of them as captains of their own vessels. While dependent on their institutions for the ship itself, its supplies and support, once they leave port they steer their own course, confident in both their seamanship and the desirability of their ultimate destination.

Bowen captures the college faculty's importance to society when he states that they

> directly influence the personal development and ideals of a large fraction of each successive generation, and they prepare these same people for a wide range of vocations including virtually all the positions of leadership and technical competence in our society. (Bowen, 1986: v)

On campus, they 'are an institution's most valuable resource – by far' (Menges, 1999: xiv). They realize both these facts and are justly proud. Their pride, however, can sometimes be mistaken for arrogance. Indeed, numerous authors have depicted faculty as the epitome of arrogance. Herbert Livesey, author of *The Professors: Who They Are, What They Do, What They Really Want and What They Need*, is positively hostile.

> A concentrated strain of arrogance flows unceasingly through the veins of the body academic. Whether in compensation for deep-seated insecurities, whether masked in mock humility or thundered about the ears of all who will listen, it is the single most pervasive characteristic of the members of the professoriate. (Livesey, 1975: 326)

He goes on to say that 'as the mandarins of our educational system, they hold themselves as something slightly more than human and therefore deserving of their lofty splendor. They are dependent upon us, yet demand inviolate insulation' (334).

Richard Sparks addresses this issue.

> I suppose some professors can be arrogant, but that's no different from any other profession. The flip side is that some students see professors as arrogant just because professors have a lot of knowledge. I'll cite an example. As you know I have a writing policy: one point off for every spelling error, one half-point off for every egregious grammar error. No exceptions. That policy has been described by many students as arrogant. I tell them simply

that my job isn't to accept them where they are, but to elevate
them to where they should be.

The fact that Livesey's book enjoyed generally good reviews upon
publication leads one to conclude that his is not a voice crying in the
wilderness, that others have experienced such haughtiness. As Thomas
English, himself a professor, notes: 'Faculty members, with their constant and occasionally unrealistic demands, may often send librarians to
the aspirin bottle' (Farber, 1974: 146).

In *The Academic Man: A Study in the Sociology of a Profession*,
Wilson provides a gentler – if still barbed – perspective to the issue.

> Every society considering itself civilized has a special class of
> persons with an institutionalized concern in that part of culture
> known as higher learning. Members of the class *homo academicus*
> flatter themselves upon differing from the common run of men by
> having their ideas and attitudes less directly and exclusively de-
> rived from simple sensory impression. Laymen in turn acknow-
> ledge this differentiation. Yet they do not always take it as a mark
> of superiority, as is evidenced by the depreciatory tone used to
> characterize certain types of problems as being of 'purely aca-
> demic interest.' (Wilson, 1995: 3)

In defense of the faculty, they have long been the subject of a great many
misconceptions. These include the notions that their working hours are
few, they do not work during the summer, they have more job security
than other professions, they receive large salaries, teaching is their only
duty, and in their ivory towers they are disconnected from the more
pressing concerns of the 'real world.' Melko characterizes such attitudes
in *A Professor's Work*.

> The gist of this criticism was that professors have cushy jobs and
> are overpaid. They teach relatively few hours, they are protected
> by tenure, they travel around the country to conferences on trips
> paid for by the state or the parents of the students. And since, like
> other professionals, they set their own standards, they protect
> their prerogatives. (Melko, 1998: 7)

Teaching at the college level, however, involves much more time than the
public imagines.

> Faculty time budgets show that, irrespective of the relative
> importance which academicians may attach to their other func-

tions, teaching makes greater time demands than any other single activity. The instructor or professor spends from six to fifteen hours weekly during the school year giving lectures and conducting classroom discussions for undergraduate or graduate students. A still greater amount of time is spent in preparation. (Wilson, 1995: 178)

Addressing the notion of an easy work week, **Jack Hettinger** estimates that he works more than fifty hours a week during a typical semester.

> I find that in addition to working Monday through Friday I often work part of Saturday and Sunday. I often work after supper. My day will start with an 8 o'clock class in the morning and I usually get here well before that.

Dan Mader, a professor in the Art Department, claims

> people don't realize how long it takes just to get the lectures and the studios ready that we teach during September through May. It's not unusual in Art History to take three or four hours to get ready for a one-hour presentation. I remember spending eight hours on one lecture and it wasn't even very good at that. You need to get your visuals together, review the outline, you put together as good a presentation as you can.

His colleague, **Elizabeth Barkley,** estimates that preparing for and teaching classes accounts for only 60 per cent of her workload. Thirty per cent of her time is devoted to additional faculty duties like advising and working on campus committees. With the remaining 10 per cent she attempts to stay current in her field and conduct scholarship.

> I'd say I'm on campus most days from 8:30 until 5:00, and then I work evenings and much of my weekend. I do have a social life and a family, too, though. I think it's easier at a large research university to come in, teach classes, have a few office hours, and then spend the rest of the day working at home, or working in the library. On this campus, though, it seems that something bleeds into the next thing, and all of a sudden it's five o'clock. I might have planned to go home at 2:00 or 3:00 to get some reading done. I thought I'd have more time during the academic year and the summer to really do class reading and explore background material. It's practically a 12-month job now and we're not on a

12-month contract. That's a big issue that we as a faculty have to confront very soon.

Tenure – a prickly topic

In addition to his other work, Dr. Gift had been chair of the university promotion and tenure committee for the last two years. It was the most sensitive committee on campus, the one most fraught with politics. The benefits of every positive decision were modest, the costs of every negative one potentially disastrous.

The preceding passage from Jane Smiley's *Moo*, a comic novel about life at a fictional university, provides as good an introduction as any to that most sensitive of academic topics, tenure. Although it has facetiously been described as 'the only feudal estate to survive the Renaissance – the modern equivalent of medieval knighthood' (Finnegan, 1996: 159), tenure is defined in *The Concise Dictionary of Education* as a 'special employment status granted to a teacher or professor such that he or she cannot be arbitrarily discharged; traditionally intended to safeguard academic freedom in teaching' (Hawes and Hawes, 1982: 228). Such status is unique to education. What many outside of academia fail to recognize, however, is how difficult tenure is to obtain. As Hostetler observes, 'the granting of tenure marks the end of the preliminary stage of a career often lasting 30 to 40 or more years' (Hostetler, 2001: 36). HERI data indicate that support for the notion that 'tenure is essential to attract the best minds in academe' is growing. While only 54 per cent of those faculty surveyed in 1995 agreed strongly or somewhat with this statement, 64 per cent concurred in 2001.

Before becoming eligible for tenure, a scholar must typically finish his undergraduate degree, his Master's degree, his doctoral class work and his dissertation. **John Trokan** describes the long road he traveled to tenure.

I did my undergraduate work at Marquette in theology, and then I continued on and did my Masters with no break. There was a break in finishing the Masters. I did the coursework, but it took me another two years to finish the language exam and write the thesis because I was working part-time during the Masters and it moved to full-time after I got the coursework done. And I had married, and so I was trying to balance and juggle all of that.

Then, there was a six year break between finishing the Master's and starting the doctoral program. I served in the Archdiocese of Milwaukee doing ministry formation work – which involved lots of part-time teaching. Teaching was the part of the job I really loved. It took three more years to finish the doctorate in ministry.

One of John's colleagues, **Jim Bodle**, recounts his formal education.

I followed what really is a pretty unusual path, but what is kind of the mold of what people say you should do. Granted, I didn't have a lot of fun. I did not do anything fun for five years [laughs]. I had the luxury of doing that because at that time I was not married and I didn't have a lot of other obligations. When I graduated with my bachelor's degree I applied to a program that focuses very heavily on recruiting students with just bachelor's degrees. That's not as common anymore, but that's the way I did it. I spent two years working on my graduate level course work, reading for the content area where I wanted to write my Master's thesis, and eventually writing a proposal, because my area in psychology is at the scientific research area of discipline. After completing all of the course work and the thesis I earned my Master's degree. By the time that I defended the Master's thesis it was two and a half years. Then I advanced to doctoral candidacy, at which time I started drawing up my content areas for my qualifying exams. That involved working with faculty on a committee to draw up a list of books and articles that would define three major content areas and then a general psychology breadth of knowledge and general methodology knowledge. Approval of the list came within half of a year, then I spent a year reading and studying from this list and taking a few more courses in experimental methodology. Then, I took my qualifying exams. This involved two days of sitting in a room for eight hours having questions passed to me under a door. I'd type away on a computer for eight hours. It was like being in prison or something! After another week or two they gave me their feedback and then gave me a three hour oral exam. They wanted me to be able to speak on any specific issues they thought were any weaknesses they'd have seen from my written answers. But they also asked completely off-the-wall questions that were just tangents of that. After that I was qualified to write a proposal for the dissertation. I finished the dissertation from beginning to end in six months. That was divine inspiration! Mine was an experimental dissertation and they tend to be shorter. Altogether, it was only 65 pages. A lot of the work was coming up with the design, compiling a comprehensive literature review to make sure that it was something that hadn't been done yet – a lot of it is in the experimental work you do to produce the document. Thankfully, I had a readily available population. Also, a lot of the work from the comprehensive exams informed how I wrote the proposal, and the body of the proposal became a significant part of the dissertation. So altogether it took me five years after my BS to get the doctoral degree.

Jim's fast-track to his PhD is an anomaly at the College of Mount St. Joseph. Consider the long and winding road of his colleague, **Tim Lynch.**

I went right from high school to Xavier University, where I majored in Philosophy and History. Typical of people my age back then, there was less of an interest to choose a degree that pointed you towards a career. There was almost an embrace of that which could not be commercialized. I was going to go to graduate school at Boston College. I was there for two weeks in American Studies, but then the monies coming from the federal government that I'd hoped would support me went to the undergraduates. When it was clear that I didn't have the financial resources I dropped out, lived in Boston for one year, moved back to Cincinnati and got a job as an audiovisual technician at Xavier. That allowed me to get the credentials to be certified to teach high school. I took advantage of their tuition remission. After one year of working at Xavier there was an opening at LaSalle High School. They ran me out of the classroom. I was very young looking. One of the other teachers told me that 'this was the worst group of bad actors ever assembled in one classroom.' By January it was pretty clear that I needed to sever my ties with LaSalle if I was going to ever have any interest in teaching again. I was able to leave in January and they let me use that time to satisfy my student teaching requirement. I spent what would have been the second semester working as a carpenter. I was really ready to give up teaching altogether because that experience had left such a bad taste in my mouth. There was an opening at Brown County Ursuline where there were only 56 students. The students were very motivated. I came into my own there. It wasn't combat in the classroom any more. I didn't make any money, but it was a wonderful experience. After two years they closed. I had the opportunity while at Brown County to teach a little at Chatfield College. That gave me a taste of college teaching, but I certainly wasn't ready at that point to go beyond teaching high school. I taught at Covington Catholic after Brown County Ursuline closed and spent seven years there. While I was there I began working part-time on a Master's degree in Humanities. It was during the summers and there was one semester that I had a reduced load. This was not a program billed as a stepping-stone program for a PhD. There was no language requirement, it was only in one discipline, and there was not a thesis per se that was required. I got that degree in 1988, after four years. Actually, I had most of the course work done by two years, but there was a project that took me longer to finish. Inertia set in. I pushed it to one side for a time. About that time I was also getting anxious for a change. I went to Highlands High School and taught there for one year. I realized then that I wasn't just looking for a change of venue, but a different challenge. I decided at that point to get a PhD at Miami University. As I think of it, it was one of those really critical decisions in my life that was based very little on reality. I was married, we already had a home, and we wanted to stay in the Cincinnati area. I was also looking forward to being a student again. I wasn't thinking much about the job market. Then after two years I did my residency and there was an opening here at the Mount. I really wasn't ready to put myself on the market, but here was a job in American Social History in my backyard and certainly I wanted to apply for it. As I look back on it I was extremely lucky because I've since been told that there were 70 or 80 other applicants. I shared an office at Miami with another one of the applicants! I took my candidacy exams the first year I was here at the Mount. Technically I wasn't even ABD [all but the dissertation]. I finished the PhD four years later. My advisor was wonderful throughout the whole process. I didn't have to start from scratch on my dissertation topic. They let me incorporate my interest in labor music along the way. My department chair was also wonderful. He never put pressure on me. I never felt pressure from the administration either, although I know some others in my situation did.

PhD in hand, a faculty member must then compete with literally hundreds of other applicants for tenure track positions. Once hired, the hard work is far from over. **Sue Johnson,** an Associate Professor of Nursing, describes her road to obtaining tenure.

> For me it was a long haul. When I first came to the Mount I didn't have a PhD. While I still had a full teaching load I had to complete my doctoral course work and my dissertation. I did take one year off where I only taught part-time in order to finish my doctoral course work. It's not easy, plus I had two small children at home, but it can be done. On the road to tenure you have to show your community service. I got hooked up with a coalition in Covington, Kentucky that dealt with pregnant teenagers, and that organization provided me with the data for my dissertation, 'Outcomes of Teen Pregnancy.' So I tried to blend what I was doing on campus with what I was doing for the doctoral work. That made it workable for me. I finished the doctoral dissertation in 1998. I think they put me on the tenure track after I finished my doctoral dissertation. The Dean gave me three years after I finished the dissertation to develop more scholarship. And she was right. It was worth the extra time because I got a couple more articles published. I started here in 1992 and I got tenure in 2001. The pre-tenure review process was very helpful and my department chair gave me some very good guidance, too. I made a few mistakes in the pre-tenure process. I had a couple of colleagues look at my portfolio before I turned it in. The main stress was thinking 'if I don't get tenure I'm losing my job.'

One of Sue's colleagues, **Alan de Courcy,** concurs. 'I think the whole tenure process is a huge stress for people. I've been on both sides of that. I've been on the tenure committee now for five years. Over and over again it hits me how stressful the whole process is.' Though guidelines vary, most institutions require faculty in tenure track positions to apply for tenure after five years of full-time service. On most campuses, a pre-tenure workshop is offered once a year to answer questions and explain the process in detail greater than that found in the institution's Faculty Handbook. Again, while details vary from institution to institution, normally a candidate's portfolio must include the following: copies of annual evaluations; self-assessment of candidate's teaching, scholarship, and academic citizenship; teaching evaluations by students and colleagues; external and internal evaluation of scholarship; and, finally, evaluation of academic citizenship. Each of these categories can be difficult to evaluate. Faculty have railed for years against the validity of student evaluations of their teaching. What constitutes scholarship – not to mention how to weigh each of these elements against others – is another difficulty. Scholarship can range from conference presentations to publications in refereed and unrefereed journals, to books, to creative works, to external guest lectures, and to grants. At the College of Mount St. Joseph, anything that expands upon what is known in that discipline or field of endeavor, breaks new ground creatively, or integrates, interprets, or applies what is known in that discipline or field of endeavor is considered to fall under the rubric of scholarship. Because it is at least quantifiable in some sense, scholarship is often the telling factor in a tenure review.

Since it practically ensures job security for life, the decision to grant tenure is not taken lightly. 'Granting tenure commits institutional resources that can total millions of dollars in salary and support' (Hostetler, 2001: 36). Nothing on campus is more politically charged than tenure review cases. 'Research and scholarly activity are frequently harshly competitive. Tenure and promotion structures pit faculty colleagues one against another, and the race is to the swift and strong' (Freedman, 1979: 8). These cases are usually heard by a committee composed of elected, tenured faculty, and the Academic Dean. Though all places of work are political to some degree, colleges and universities have long enjoyed a reputation as being especially so. Falk provides a good definition of politics as it applies to the campus.

> If the word 'politics' is meant as the manipulation of other people, the effort to influence others in one's favor, the effort to attain the power to punish one's enemies and reward one's friends, then 'politics' is indeed all of these things. (Falk, 1990: 13)

He goes on to state that 'it has been estimated that 80 per cent to 90 per cent of employees who lose their jobs are not fired because of incompetence but because of office politics. The same holds true of the failure to gain acceptance of a dissertation' (26), and, we can infer, the failure to gain tenure.

Finally, it's worth noting that the tenure process can be especially difficult for female faculty members. A recent study found that compared to their male peers, women who achieve tenure are more often single or divorced, and have had fewer children than they would have liked (Mason and Goulden, 2002). Since females pursuing doctorates now outnumber males, academe must find ways to address such an important issue.

Other faculty stressors

Obtaining tenure is only one stressor facing faculty. Menges has identified the following factors: (1) a staggering workload; (2) balancing teaching and scholarship; (3) advising; (4) burn out; (5) committee work; and (6) administrivia (Menges, 1999). These elements vary greatly from individual to individual, but usually center around a lack of necessary time. When asked about major sources of stress, faculty members I interviewed repeatedly cited a lack of time.

Alan de Courcy:

> There's never enough time to really be prepared. Now, how much of that is an illusion, I'm really not sure. But with committee work, class prep, and other things like that you just don't have enough time.

Annette Muckerheide:

> I don't have enough time. There are constant interruptions. I can't get anything done here. It's a lack of time to really think. It's too much to do in too little time. I'm teaching a full load of classes – 12 credits, sometimes 15 – and I'm the chair on top of all of that. Then, we're expected to do scholarship and there are the committees, the endless committees. Being a department chair is middle management. I've got the administration on one hand, faculty on the other. And then I've got the students. I end up advising the hard ones. In other words, the people who come here as transfers, who change majors because they're failing in one major, or the people who have asked for a different adviser.

Jim Bodle:

> It seems to me that faculty serve a role that's in part administrative and in part teaching, and this is paired against the demand for scholarship, advising students, running a department or program, and service demands such as being on committees. It's a lot to juggle all at the same time. To do any one of these effectively is pulling time away from something else you'd rather be doing.

HERI data largely confirm this anecdotal evidence, identifying the following sources of job-related stress: time pressures (83 per cent); lack of personal time (78 per cent); institutional demands and red tape (71 per cent); teaching load (65 per cent); and committee work (62 per cent). Research or publishing demands finished well down the list (47 per cent), as did the review and promotion process (also 47 per cent). Seventy per cent of faculty reported that 'keeping up with information technology' is a major source of stress. Menges notes that rather than saving them time, the new technology 'has instead placed significantly greater demands on them: by all reported accounts, the faculty workload has increased substantially as faculty scramble to infuse technology into their courses' (Menges, 1999: xii).

The College of Mount St. Joseph has a universal (sometimes called 'ubiquitous') computing requirement. All entering freshmen are required to purchase a laptop PC (nicknamed Merlins). The goal of this program is to equip each student with the technology skills expected of today's working professionals, while preparing him for a lifetime of learning. An **anonymous faculty member** comments on the benefits and drawbacks of using technology in the classroom.

> I love technology. I was one of the first faculty on campus to get my website up and I was very excited about it. I still am, but the downside of technology in the classroom has not yet really begun to be dealt with. I think there's a real question if in the end the downside will outweigh the benefits. I think it can be every bit as much a distraction as it can help. Every teacher I talk to now asks 'what do you do to get your students to not use their laptops in class?' My policy on this – and I put this in my syllabus – is that unless I've told you to take out your computer, the computer needs to be closed – without exceptions. Now I've had students come to me and say 'we paid for this, and now you're telling me we can't use it?' I had no good answer to that other than 'yes, that is what I'm telling you. I didn't tell you you had to buy it. You need to take it up with the people who did'. I think some of that is that the people who pushed the technology are not teachers. They see that as valuable but they aren't the ones who have to use it in the classroom. I love the bulletin board (WebCT), but I find the best use of it is outside class, in particular my graduate classes that don't meet very often.

An **anonymous colleague** offers her assessment.

> I think students probably need to understand in a broader way
> what technology can do rather than just learning how to use a
> particular resource. We are a wired campus. All my writing and
> speech classes are totally computer-based. I give them links they
> can go to, they submit assignments electronically. I use WebCT in
> what I think is a balanced way. It can be used so intensely that it
> becomes a burden. I use it to post syllabi, get discussion groups
> going, and even set up special discussion groups among students
> so that they don't always have to meet. The nice thing is when
> they use it for things that aren't required, to communicate to one
> another or to share ideas. In my journalism classes the technology
> is very helpful. Their assignment might be to go to a newspaper
> online and then talk to their group about why they chose that
> particular paper. It's transformed the class completely. One
> downside of technology is that students expect you to instantly
> respond to them when they send you something electronically.
> They become very impatient. They're used to using Instant Mes-
> senger, text messaging on phones, and so on.

Jeff Hillard concurs:

> I've seen a generation of students coming through now that is more
> demanding of our expertise. They want their information and then
> they want to fly. They don't want it fifty minutes after the class
> starts; they want it ten minutes after the class starts. If you don't
> deliver, or you don't catch what they need, they'll turn you off.

'Technology is at least a double-edged sword,' notes **Jim Bodle.**

> One of the problems that you run into with technology is that I
> don't know that we all have sufficiently adapted what we do to
> really take advantage of the technology. Sometimes students just
> get bored and here's this thing in front of them, and the profes-
> sor's not really asking them to do anything with it, but there are
> competing temptations. I find that if you are able to deliberately
> tell students to do something in class, then the inappropriate use
> will go down. In my Introduction to Psychology course, for in-
> stance, we used to do a lot of these little surveys that were a very
> short personality inventory, and the student would have to do that

manually in class and score it and that would begin the discussion in class about the topic. Carolyn Boland [the College's webmaster] has helped me be able to make those into instantly scoring HTML documents. Now I can say, 'link to the WebCT calendar today. The survey's there. Complete it now and it will give you the score.' Right there they're doing something that's saving paper, giving them the instant score, and it's using technology to do the very thing I wanted them to do. So some of the responsibility lies with the faculty member adapting to the technology. Students can find all sorts of ways of outsmarting us.

John Trokan lists some advantages of the new technology.

I embrace it because I see it as a marvelous tool in terms of enhancing your work. I've done a lot of PowerPoint authoring and used WebCT quite often, and I enjoy doing that. It really has deepened the learning and made it much more accessible. It can also be utilized in regard to on-and off-campus use. I'm still looking for new ways to change and adapt and use it in the classroom.

Another source of faculty stress is the growing trend in American society to hold institutions of higher education more accountable for their product. **Elizabeth Barkley:**

It's a slippery slope from what's happening in grade school. They might not be holding us accountable for things that are valid. It's started in primary and secondary schools and now it's coming up. See, I think a lot of things that happen in higher education are not measurable, tied to learning outcomes and performance indicators. That's a really scary trend, to think that we can reduce a college education – which used to be this mind-opening, broadening, liberal arts, life-changing experience – into checking off skills rather than developing habits of mind. I think the accrediting bodies are feeling pressure from consumers and politicians, and it's tied into the cost of education. As you pay more and more you want to get something for your money that's got to be measurable. I don't know what's driving up the cost of education. Maybe it's all the technology. It's scary to me that so many students are not going to be able to afford an education, or that they're going to be so in debt by the time they graduate, that they're not going to be able to buy a home or raise children.

An **anonymous colleague** sees the movement towards greater account-ability as symptomatic of another trend:

> The state legislatures want university professors to account for their hours in the same way that corporations want their employees to, as if we were some kind of machines working on producing something. Which is another source of tension for me, our industrial notion of education.

It is a gross understatement that dealing with college administrators can often be stressful for faculty members. An examination of this difficulty reveals the sometimes conflicted nature of the faculty psyche. 'Faculty wish and do not wish strong leadership' (Adams, 1988: 16). One of the faculty antinomies Adams describes is the feeling that they *are* the university, yet they are also its employees. 'People paid are responsible to the people who pay, even though it is recognized by those who pay that in this case the relationship is a special one and that only limited control and interference is tolerable' (16). The second antinomy Adams identifies is that 'the Administration is the master of the faculty; the administration is the servant of the faculty' (16). This philosophical struggle was played out in a Supreme Court case in 1979 involving Yeshiva University in New York. Speaking for the majority decision, Justice Powell wrote:

> The authority [of faculty members] in academic matters is abso-lute. They decide what courses will be offered, when they will be scheduled, and to whom they will be taught. They debate and determine teaching methods, grading policies, and matriculation standards. They effectively decide which students will be admit-ted, retained, and graduated. On occasion their views have determined the size of the student body, the tuition to be charged, and the location of a school. When one considers the function of a university, it is difficult to imagine decisions more managerial than these. (National Labor Relations Board, 1979)

In his minority opinion, Justice Brennan wrote that

> Authority is lodged in the administration, and a formal chain of command runs from a lay governing board down through uni-versity officers to individual faculty members and students ... The University always retains the ultimate decision-making authority.

Speaking further on the topic, an **anonymous faculty member** would like to see colleges emulate a recent trend in industry.

I thought the administration at the College would recognize better how faculty spend their time. I feel like there should be a great deal more flexibility in the way that classes are scheduled vis-à-vis the talents and skills the professors bring to the college. Look at how companies are changing. They're recognizing the individual talents of their employees. They're giving them more liberty to do those things they do especially well. You used to sit in your seat, take orders from the top, and the product is produced. Now companies are realizing that good leadership comes when leaders allow their people more room and flexibility. I don't feel that many professors here have comparable opportunities.

Richard Sparks notes another source of tension between faculty and the administration.

The goals a Dean or an administrator might have aren't the same as those which a faculty member might have. An administrator tends to see a faculty member as one who is here solely to serve the needs of the College. Whereas the faculty member – especially one who does a lot of scholarship – sees his or her role as not only serving the College, but as someone who is a scholar to the external community, whose job it is to write and disseminate research. Too often – and maybe this only occurs at a small college; I've never been at a university – the total focus tends to be on serving the needs of the College.

With all its stressors, however, life as a faculty member is one most would not give up. The majority would undoubtedly agree with Boice that they could not

imagine a lifestyle with more opportunities for satisfaction and growth. Think of it: professors work mainly at their own pace and on their own schedules; they generally do the things they like most, such as reading and thinking. They have many off days and long vacations, including entire summers, if they wish. Their involvement as teachers and as scholars provides a self-education that can surpass all expectations. Their interactions with students and colleagues can be stimulating and fun; indeed, the depth and worth of such friendships may be unmatched in other professions. (Boice, 2000: 1)

The HERI study substantiates this statement. Forty-nine per cent of respondents indicated that they would definitely still want to be a college professor if they were to begin their career again. A further 33 per cent answered that they probably would. Twelve per cent were unsure and only 6 per cent responded that they would probably or definitely choose another profession (Lindblom, 2002).

Most look on teaching as a calling. **John Trokan,** for example, states

> It is a vocation and teaching is something I do with my whole person. It's a 12-month commitment in terms of nurturing the skills I have and bringing them into every class I teach. I look at it as a covenant. When we sit down in class with the syllabus, we're really partnering in this endeavor. I have to do everything I can to be as knowledgeable to facilitate that learning as I possibly can. Some days I do that well, some days not so well, but the commitment to continue to try to do that is always there.

A colleague, **Peg McPeak,** describes one of the joys that can be found in the job. 'The satisfying thing about teaching is seeing the students come to appreciate – they don't have to like it – something, to see that light go on and have them think "yes, that makes sense."' **Ron White** adds that 'Teaching for me is fun. If I were a millionaire I'd still teach and do scholarship.'

Who are librarians? Who are faculty?

Dozens of articles have been written about whether or not academic librarians should have faculty status. While this issue seems to preoccupy many of my peers, I believe that a more important question regarding the health of an academic library is to determine the extent to which faculty respect librarians and the role they play in the educational process. Do librarians feel inferior to faculty members? While their efforts to attain faculty status do not, I think, reflect 'the deleterious psychological effects of a repugnant self-image' (Biggs, 1981: 192), I believe that some novice academic librarians are at least intimidated by faculty. Adams notes that librarians 'inhabit a shadowy ground between faculty and staff' (Adams, 1988: 22). They 'seem to regard themselves as the most shamelessly exploited and they perplex those functionaries who must create tables of organization' (22). Certainly one cannot ignore the fact that most academic librarians lack PhDs, and thus, one might argue, some status in the eyes of faculty. Hardesty makes another important distinction between the two groups. While librarians prize the attainment of knowledge, faculty emphasize its application. 'Faculty culture values autonomy, research and publication ideals, and the pursuit of knowledge for its own sake' (Hardesty, 1988: 67).

And yet how similar the two groups are as well! 'Since people tend to respect and to interact more easily with those who are most similar to them, librarians and faculty are natural partners in academic endeavors' (Scherdin, 2002: 237). Scherdin's statement prefaces her discussion of the similarities and differences between faculty and librarian personality types, as measured by the Myers-Briggs Type Indicator (MBTI), the tool long recognized as the premier measure of personality types. MBTI measures four personality preferences based on the following dichotomies: Introversion–Extroversion; Intuition–Sensing; Thinking–Feeling; and Judging–Perception. Scherdin found that librarians' preferences were as follows:

- introversion (I) 63 per cent;
- intuition (N) 60 per cent;
- thinking (T) 64 per cent;
- judging (J) 63 per cent.

Scores found in the Data Bank of the Center for the Application of Psychological Type show that faculty also fit the INTJ profile. 'These similarities in preferences among academic librarians and faculty stand in stark contrast to the general population. The types found most frequently among the academics are found least frequently in the general population' (Scherdin, 2002: 243).

So what does this tell us? 'Introverts, when paired with other Introverts, feel a great depth of commitment for and from each other' (Scherdin, 2002: 247). Individual conversations yield more results than group interaction. What more could one possibly ask for in an educational partner? Great vitality results when Intuitives communicate with each other. Thinking types share a focus on tasks and find common ground in solutions to challenges. 'Because they depersonalize conflict, there will be a minimal amount of hurt feelings among Thinking types' (247). Judging types clarify responsibility for tasks and typically have no difficulty in making decisions.

Still, problems between the two groups persist. Not every faculty member can be described as 'library-friendly.' As part of his dissertation research, Hardesty created the Library Educational Attitude Scale (LEAS). Some 234 faculty members at four Indiana institutions of varying size (ranging from smallest, Earlham, to largest, Purdue) completed this 30-item survey. Based on their responses, Hardesty was able to identify four faculty types. The first he called 'library-resistant.' They believed that librarians should educate students about the library. The second, 'library-minimization,' recognized that the library does play a small role in the education of undergraduates. While most students will use the library only as a place to study, the 'best and brightest' will make some use of the library and its services. These faculty were still unwilling to help students use the library. The third type, dubbed 'library-traditionalists,' felt that library staff should inspire students to use the library, but not necessarily instruct them how to use it. The fourth group, 'library-active,' supported 'the active involvement of the library in undergraduate education' (Hardesty, 1991: 46). They saw librarians as full partners in the educational process and indicated a willingness to work with them to teach students how to better use the library.

In my everyday life as director of a small college library I have encountered representatives of each of these groups, although I tend to classify them more informally as library-friendly, occasional users, and non-users. This last group is usually made up of faculty from disciplines like Mathematics or Accounting where library use is minimal for both teacher and student. Some departments whose faculty do use the library prefer to use a department member as liaison to handle all matters with the library, thus largely eliminating the need for others in the department to contact it. Library-friendly faculty are usually good and frequent communicators. These tend to be faculty from the humanities (History, Philosophy, and Literature) and other disciplines that use the library quite often themselves and thus see student use of the facility as vital. It is the group I label occasional users that probably should merit most of our attention. They have realized the usefulness of the library, but may need some additional prodding to learn more about our services, make greater use of them, and encourage their students to darken our doorway more often than they already do. 'I need reminding again and again and again' (Stahl, 1997: 134), admits one faculty member. 'Therefore, expect me to ask you repeatedly for the same information; if you find subtle ways to remind me about resources, it's probably not overkill' (134). On the other hand, Stahl notes that such proactivity should be 'tempered with an acute sense of when to back off' (133).

Interested faculty will ask questions about library services, and we must listen well. While it is a truism, it is useful to reiterate that effective communication is the only means we have to together serve our students more effectively. Dick Raspa, a professor at Wayne State University, and Dane Ward, coordinator of instruction services at Central Michigan University, have identified five qualities that promote successful collaboration. The first, 'passion,' is what you bring to the table, what led you to choose a career in higher education. Given that their ultimate goals are similar – educating young people to help shape a better society – librarians and faculty can surely find common ground. The second, 'persistence,' is a particular favorite of mine. A dogged approach to pursuing knowledge has often served as my substitute for genius. Collaboration will not always be easy, so we must both be prepared to persevere. The third, 'playfulness,' may sound odd until more fully explained. 'Being playful does not mean not taking work seriously or trivializing our enterprise. Rather, playfulness is the capacity to engage an enterprise deeply – mind, heart, and spirit – all parts of us brought into the action of the moment' (Raspa and Ward, 2000: 9). The fourth, 'project,' simply means that our collaboration must have a focus. Fifth and finally, we must be willing to 'promote' our projects (with passion, persistence, and playfulness). Though Raspa and Ward recognize the fact that each camp shares responsibility for collaborative efforts, they suggest that librarians take the necessary first step. Again, this makes perfect sense to me. Though I'm happy to report that many are willing converts, collaborating with librarians is something faculty think about rarely and act on even less frequently.

The recent literature suggests that academic librarians have taken this proactive role to heart. 'Computerization and digitalization – more than anything else in the history of academic librarianship – has forced librarians to redefine their roles' (Raspa and Ward, 2000: 21). Faculty are having as much trouble as non-academics keeping up with the information explosion, including, of course, learning new library research skills.

> It has become the livelihood of academic librarians to stay abreast of the techniques and strategies of electronic searching. Because they are the first to interface with these databases (often before they

have been released for public use), librarians have indeed become campus experts on modern electronic research methodology (21).

Most information sharing of this kind concerns the concept of information literacy. So rampant has this movement become that it will warrant its own chapter in this book.

Service or servitude?

It is safe, I believe, to characterize librarians as people who want to help others. In dealing with various faculty requests, however, the academic librarian must sometimes wonder where to draw the line, where to make a distinction between providing good service and becoming the faculty member's servant. Pennsylvania State University makes the following distinctions between these two concepts.

> Those in service are subordinate only in the sense that servers watch over and maintain activities which need their careful attention. Servitude, on the other hand, is when the ego is under the thralldom of another. Servitude is more akin to slavery or bondage. (Available online at: *https://courses.worldcampus.psu.edu/welcome/hrim315/x02pw/samplecontent.shtml*)

Librarian Christine Larson summarizes the issue well in an article titled 'What I Want in a Faculty Member'.

> As a librarian, I have expectations about faculty abilities and behaviors in the library. I personally expect that anyone with a Ph.D., who has had to research, write, and publish, has a basic familiarity with the literature in his or her field and the basic research tools used to search it. I also expect that faculty can and want to do their own research for course preparation and publications and that their disciplinary expertise and judgment are essential to doing this well. I do not, however, expect a faculty member to know the old, familiar research tools in their latest electronic manifestation, nor the tools for a strange discipline they suddenly find themselves needing to use. I don't expect faculty to have finely developed, intuitive skills that enable them to sniff out the real source in a problematic citation or construct a complex query for an unfriendly database. I don't

even expect a faculty member to make a ten-minute walk across campus for a tidbit of information that a librarian can quickly and easily deliver by phone or e-mail. I certainly don't expect familiarity with a rapidly changing information environment that has even librarians' heads spinning! Librarians should help provide faculty with guidance, assistance, and instruction for general research needs and specialized research for difficult problems outside of a faculty member's expertise. I expect faculty to recognize librarians not as research servants, but as professional colleagues who provide services appropriate to each part of the campus community, including teaching faculty. (Larson, 1998: 261)

Regarding service of any kind, I have always endorsed the proverbial motto: 'He gives twice who gives quickly.' Mark Cain, writing from an instructional technology perspective, provides four additional rules of good service that can easily be applied to the library or any other department supporting campus faculty:

- 'We should make things easier for people, so that students can get educated. If we get in the way of that, either with procedures or systems design or attitude, we're not delivering the best service' (Cain, 2002: 7–8).

- 'We should make things easier on ourselves only after we've made them easier on the customer' (8).

- 'Say yes or provide an alternative. A flat-out no is never appropriate' (8).

- 'Empathize with the user. That and a genuine desire to help motivate the good service provider' (8).

Cautionary tales from librarians

The following experiences illustrate some of the ways the faculty–librarian relationship can go wrong. A library director from a small college in North Carolina recounts one such tale.

The institution was a small, liberal arts college, a fairly young school, and underfunded. With a history of neglect, the library budget did not stretch to meet resource needs. We had a new faculty member teaching business and marketing classes, and although I had met him (we have a brief orientation program for new faculty members) and explained book order policies and procedures and offered to discuss resource needs for his classes, he had never responded. The professor was African and his experience had been at larger institutions with larger libraries. He acted like he should be treated as king ('your wish is my command'), and he seldom responded to my calls. My first sign of trouble was in September when (frustrated and angry) students came in asking how they could find certain peer-reviewed journals. Although our collections in business were stronger than in other areas, and we had access to over 20 full-text, peer-reviewed journals through online databases, we did not have the specific titles this faculty member recommended. We identified some articles and ordered them through interlibrary loan, but my memory is that the professor had given students only a couple of days or a weekend on the assignment, so ILL was not a satisfactory response. I called and e-mailed the professor asking to talk with him about the resources his students needed, but I got no response. The next week, these students were back telling me that their professor was saying they shouldn't bother with our library, they should just drive directly to the library at UNC-Chapel Hill or Duke to find what they needed! (These institutions are about 1–2 hours from our campus, and many of our students had neither transportation nor the time – given work and family commitments – for such excursions.) Students received little or no credit for the assignment if the professor did not accept the articles they found, so students with strong grade-point averages were worried about the impact on their grades. Again, I tried contacting the professor. He wanted the library to subscribe to *Strategic Management Journal* at a cost of over $1,000 per year, when our total periodical budget was about $46,000 and not increasing. I wondered why the available print and full-text titles were insufficient, and why students were telling me that he would not accept full-text titles from online databases. I succeeded in getting a meeting with the professor and showed him how to use the relevant online databases in business. I agreed to add the requested journal with next year's subscriptions and to pick up the current year in microfilm, but noted that these would not be available immediately. The professor seemed mollified and made no comments to me, but he continued to tell students not to bother with our library – just to go to Duke or

Chapel Hill. This approach was particularly frustrating to me because the college was preparing for its ten-year reaccreditation visit, and I was well aware that we had a responsibility to serve our students and could not simply send them elsewhere.

A librarian now working in Florida reports:

> I was a tenure-track librarian at Louisiana State University and responsible for instruction and collection development in Education. An Education faculty member, a library school faculty member, and I contributed to a grant proposal for a combined school and public library in a very poor Louisiana parish. The first submission of the grant wasn't funded. The next year the proposal was successfully funded in the amount of $1.6 million. My name and the library faculty member's name had somehow dropped from the grant. The Education faculty member refused to return my calls or answer e-mails. I finally got the school district superintendent to write a letter stating that I had contributed to the grant. Since then, I've been very reluctant to engage in faculty collaborations.

A collection management coordinator details two worrying encounters with a faculty member

> I've had two incidents involving the same professor at a small, private, religiously affiliated college in the South. He was a Management professor, a retired Air Force Lt. Colonel, and he definitely was used to being in charge. (1) Despite numerous signs on the doors and personal attempts to be friendly, we never could break him of the habit of wandering around the building with his dripping ice cream cone and coming behind the circulation desk to check out the reserve materials without asking. (2) He checked out a book and did not return it. After waiting for the appropriate time to pass and following our policies, we refused him further library privileges. He was furious that we were holding him responsible for the book, since he had 'lent it to a student to be helpful, and it wasn't his problem if the student failed to return it.' He even wrote to the Vice President for Academic Affairs (VPAA) protesting our policy. (The VPAA just rolled his eyes.) Also, he would turn in incomplete and/or simply incorrect ILL forms and library request forms in illegible handwriting.

Maintaining a user-friendly reserve collection demands good communication between faculty and library staff. One librarian confirms this.

I work in the reserves department at an academic library and had a difficult situation with a faculty member soon after I started my position there. The faculty member wanted to put several photocopied articles on reserve for one of his classes. He had used those same articles a few semesters earlier and was under the impression that the articles were physically still at the library. While I did find written evidence that the articles had been on reserve a few semesters earlier, the articles were not at the library any longer. The reserves department contacts faculty members at the end of each semester to find out if they want reserves material returned to them or if they plan to use it again, in which case it can remain at the library. Contact attempts are made several times per e-mail and also per phone. If there is no reply, the material is taken off reserve and placed in the faculty member's mail box or delivered personally to the faculty member's department office. My supervisor assured me that my predecessor had been very meticulous in his job and had often personally returned reserve material. Also, it was virtually impossible that such a large number of articles had disappeared all at once. In regard to this information and the fact that class reserve articles are not exactly the most burning issue that faculty members have on their mind, I concluded that the articles had been returned to the faculty member and that he just did not remember this fact and had consequently misplaced them. However, the faculty member was highly upset and kept emphasizing that the library had lost his articles. I, on the other hand, tried to focus on finding a solution so that the articles could be placed on reserve again. Our normal policy is that faculty have to fill out an online request form for each article and provide us with photocopies of all articles, even if the library owns the journal from which the articles are taken. At this point, however, I offered to make the faculty member photocopies at the library of those we owned, and to fill out all the request forms for the others for him. While he did drop off all the photocopies himself at the library shortly thereafter, I still had to fill out all the requests. This was a very unpleasant experience since the faculty member kept accusing the library of losing his articles, while I was virtually certain that this was not the case. It definitely helped that I tried to focus on a solution rather than trying to determine who was to blame. While I did have my opinion about this, I never expressed my suspicion that the faculty member had misplaced the articles. I tried to focus on good customer service and a fast resolution of the problem in the best interest of the students, even if this meant more work for me.

A science librarian relates a lengthy tale of an interlibrary loan request gone astray.

It all started a few months after being hired with a professor who needed some esoteric information. He gave me the typical reference information: 'Well, I'm not sure, but I think the author is ...' After several hours of tracking incorrect citations, misguided hunches, and several dead ends, I found the information he wanted. I sent the professor the correct citation, where I found it, and how to order it via interlibrary loan. Several days later, I found out that the ILL department was having difficulties in obtaining this material. Normally, I would let the ILL department handle this situation by way of their 'canned' e-mail responses, but the faculty member seemed to really need this information in a hurry. So I tracked down the e-mail address of the librarians of the lending institution and sent them a message with the hope that they could provide some assistance, to which I received no reply. I decided to inform the professor that the library was unable to borrow the material – this in addition to the ILL department's standard e-mail response – and provided the lending institution's contact information in case he wanted to pursue getting the information himself. I pointed out a phone number and fax number I pulled from the institution's website, and suggested calling them since they weren't responding to e-mail. Two weeks later, I received an e-mail from the professor asking if I should try phoning these two numbers or if he should try. It had been two weeks since our last e-mail, and I had assumed that he either tried calling himself or had simply given up. A few hours later, I happened to meet the professor face to face, and the topic of the phone call came up. After discussing the situation, I explained that I shouldn't make the phone call because I didn't speak the language, the library had already attempted to borrow the material, and I didn't have the authority to order material via interlibrary loan even if they were willing to lend the material. I tried to tactfully say that the library had reached the end of the rope with no other options, and the rest was up to him if he wished to continue. I did, however, offer to resend the e-mail message (which I did and received no response). A few days later, the professor wrote back and stated that I gave him a fax number to call. I politely pointed out that there were two numbers: one for fax and one for phone. I asked if he tried the second number – he hadn't. A few minutes later, I received a copied e-mail message from the professor to the ILL Manager stating that I asked him to 'follow up on his own,' and after phoning the correct phone number discovered that they were nine hours ahead. Coming in early or late to make an international call was 'impractical' for him. Could the ILL Manager do this for him? I was surprised by this request, but thought that the ILL Manager could handle the response since it was addressed to him. A month and a half later I received yet another e-mail from the same professor. This time the subject on the e-mail was entitled 'Expectations for Performance.' It was copied to the Library Director and the Associate Director. It basically read that he wanted to meet in person sometime to get my full job description. He believed that I was not doing my job and wanted to know what to expect from me so that he could know what to do on his own in the future. There was also an open invitation to bring either the Library Director or Associate Director to the meeting. After taking a little time to cool down, I talked to the Library Director and Associate Director. They had read the e-mail from the faculty member, but were not surprised by his request. Apparently, this faculty member had a similar history with several other librarians, and that he was really 'pushing to get his way.' They reviewed my e-mail dialog with the professor (I save all of my e-mails), and were impressed with the amount and quality of work I put into this consultation. The Associate Director offered to be a mediator if I wanted, but suggested talking to the faculty member individually at first. Both said that they backed me up completely. When I finally met the professor, we were able to patch things up quickly and fairly painlessly. In turn, I found that he didn't know how the library worked, or any of the library's policies. I discovered too that while he was trying to get the information he needed for research, he wasn't trying to push people around to get his way.

The many morals to this story: (1) Through this single reference consultation, I learned a great deal. I found that good communication is essential for success, and good communication isn't simply relaying what you know to another person, but interpreting and putting it in a way they can understand. (2) I also learned to keep your supervisors up to speed on problems you may encounter, since they may be a staunch defender on your behalf. (3) Save your e-mail communications because they provide great documentation between two parties. (4) Beware of assumptions because they may be incorrect. If you are not certain about something, make sure to ask. (5) Remember that the only stupid question is the one not asked. (6) Avoid burning the bridges of relationships, as you may need to cross them sometime in the future. (7) Positive encouragement goes a long way in times of trouble.

Anne Woodsworth, a former library director and now Dean of the Palmer School of Library and Information Science, relates the following anecdotes.

One professor, upon learning that part of the collection in her discipline would be placed in compact shelving, vowed to throw herself into the shelves and have her colleagues close them up. Instead of working with the library staff, she and her colleagues complained in a delegation to the provost. Did we change plans for what was to be placed in the compact shelves? You betcha. But I had made enemies. Another faculty member was told through a routine notice that his library privileges would be suspended unless he paid his outstanding library fines (an action outlined in his union contract). He stormed into my office, called me a #!&%^%! policewoman, and threatened to get me fired. When threats failed, he tried to bribe me with a weekend (with him) in his New York apartment. (Needless to say that this incident took place before current sensitivities to sexual harassment, and, yes, I said 'No thank you,' to his 'invitation.') When these creative tactics did not result in cancellation of his fine, he grumbled to the university president, who, fortunately, had read the union contract and upheld both the fine and the punishment. Both the president and I made an enemy. (Woodsworth, 1998: 54)

Helpful hints and advice from faculty

Zoe Toft, a linguistics instructor at the School of Oriental and African Studies, University of London, cautions librarians that 'Academics are, even at the best of times, not used to having to rely on other people and, if promises fail to materialize, can easily give up or go elsewhere' (Toft, 2004: 43). A former assistant in a university library, Toft was predisposed to work with librarians in her desire to create a list of electronic linguistics resources she and her students could use. Nevertheless, to begin the project she compiled her own list.

> I found resources by asking fellow academics, both by e-mail and through online forums, using subject-specific portals I was already aware of and signing up to alerting systems such as Google alert, Humbul and those set up by publishing houses. These were tried and tested research strategies from my time as a student and so they came naturally (42).

Eventually she sent her list to the library and, after a librarian made some corrections, it was added to the library's web page. She suggests that librarians must raise their profiles so that faculty are more aware of the kind of help they can provide. Simultaneously, however, they must remember that most faculty have a 'desire to work alone and to be self-reliant' (43). Her article illustrates well how difficult it can be for faculty to work with librarians even when the inclination to do so exists.

In their efforts to improve collaboration between faculty and librarians at Eastern Kentucky University, the library staff wrote a grant to raise sufficient money to host an overnight retreat. Their rationale was basic: 'Teaching faculty needed librarians for assignment development; for determining appropriate levels of research; and for learning about new ways of doing research. Librarians needed faculty members to remain viable in a time when electronic ease threatens the existence of the profession' (Cooper and Gardner, 2001: 23). The event was the culmination of a metamorphosis of sorts for the library staff that saw them 'shed the stereotype of the passive storekeeper of knowledge' (23) and transform into proactive partners of their faculty. Faculty selected by the library staff were keen to participate as well. The day of the retreat, librarians brainstormed as to how their job descriptions might change so that more proactive tasks might become possible. The faculty members arrived for dinner, then the two groups talked informally. The following day librarians paired up with faculty to discuss individual projects. Not all of the projects involved library instruction. One, for example, called for a librarian's presence in the campus Writing Center. Whatever their variations, however, both groups concluded that the projects would ultimately make their professional lives easier. Librarians will 'be better prepared to help students with assignments' and 'faculty will be forced to evaluate resources before designing an assignment, which in turn will equate to better student projects' (25).

Ed Holley (1985) has identified the following qualities academic librarians must possess to succeed:

- a background in the history and development of higher education;
- an appreciation for the history of scholarship and learning;
- an understanding of how knowledge is obtained in various disciplines;
- an ability to evaluate research findings.

I asked College of Mount St. Joseph faculty members what qualities they think are important to a successful academic librarian.

Mary Kay Fleming:

> I think one thing that I would hope they'd do is to do what you all do – be full partners of the faculty, from committee work, to speaking up at meetings. You've done a good job of fully integrating it with teaching, but it might take a person who's aggressively pursuing that to do it. In other words, I could imagine a librarian who kind of hung back and thought 'when they need me, they'll visit.' I don't think you all do that and I don't think you should. Some new faculty might not come into the situation knowing that you're full partners, but here they will form that impression very quickly. So I would hope that librarians in training develop the mindset that they are full partners, that they deserve to be, and that they should look for opportunities to make that point to faculty.

Richard Sparks:

> They should be technologically savvy. A lot of professors aren't. So be patient with us. Walking us through things step by step is so valuable, like you did with me. Now I can do these things by myself. The other thing is that sometimes we don't know how to

ask for what we want. I may have an overarching concept of what I want, but the librarian needs to be able to narrow it down. You know the sources well and I don't. Just because we know something in a particular topic area, it doesn't mean that we know where to look for it or how to find it.

Elizabeth Barkley:

I think if you're aiming this book at future librarians they should really consider working in an academic library because it's a very energizing atmosphere to be in. It's a stable, returning population compared to, let's say, that of a public library. In a library like ours you can build peer relationships. I think once people have had interactions with the librarians they gain great respect for them. We see them as support, but we don't look down on them. It's a different job on campus that can be a great help to us.

Jeff Hillard:

You have to be people-friendly and a good communicator about what the library can offer, what new resources it has. I think a challenge for librarians is to demystify the old notion of a library as hallowed ground. You want this image to remain in some ways, but you want to create an image of a library as more user-friendly than it has been in the past.

Jim Bodle:

It's important for librarians to understand the campus that they're working on, especially on the smaller campuses they need to be willing to be responsive to the faculty's needs. It can be difficult being on a small campus and trying to do a piece of research and not being able to find an article or a book. That's not something we have an issue with here. If we ask for something it's there, faster than you ask for it half the time. But I know that's not always the case on some campuses. On a small campus your collection will resemble the faculty on your campus. One of the biggest roles a librarian can play today is educating some faculty as to the different ways of accessing some material. A lot of older faculty may not know how useful a full-text online source might be, that that can be a better way of meeting the needs of your faculty than actually subscribing to the journal in print. The library's resources really are your faculty's lifeline – 70 per cent to

80 per cent anyway – to the community beyond that college. Today what this means is less having a good collection and more having a good system of interlibrary loan.

Conclusions

When working with faculty, bear in mind that they deserve our respect. They have cleared a great number of hurdles to get where they are; many are yet to face the greatest hurdle: achieving tenure. Librarians must respect faculty, but not fear them. They must remember that most faculty are used to working independently; that they are very busy; that they recognize and respect the library's mission but may not always have time to strictly follow its procedures. Many faculty are embracing technological developments, but others still prefer time-tested pedagogical methods. Since they hold others to their own high standards and realize their importance in the institution, faculty members can come off as demanding, or even arrogant. They can be sensitive to perceived slights. Obviously then, faculty can be a challenge to work with. Just as clearly, however, no other group has a greater influence over the student body and its use of the library. Finally, the faculty represent a constant in academe. Librarians who wish to succeed in this environment must learn to understand faculty characteristics and concerns in order to work with them effectively.

2

Collection development and faculty

'It does not matter how many books you may have, but whether they are good or not.' – Seneca

Collection development has long been recognized as one aspect of academic librarianship in which faculty–librarian collaboration is paramount. 'An intractable, apparently eternal problem plaguing academic libraries is the unevenness of faculty commitment to collection building' (Biggs, 1981: 188). Common sense tells us that as the subject experts, faculty should have a say in determining which books, videos, DVDs, CDs, and journals should fill library shelves. Librarians, however, are sometimes more in tune than their faculty colleagues with the types of materials students request help in locating. They have a better understanding of the parameters of the entire library collection instead of just one segment of it. Librarians 'see the collection in a way that the individual faculty member or department is not likely to see it' (Carter, 1974: 63). They also often have collection development duties included in their job description and are willing to devote time to the practice.

A library's collection development policy is the foundation upon which all selection decisions should be based. Once the document has been drafted, faculty should be invited to examine it and make suggested changes. Posting it on your library's website is an easy way to make it publicly available. After a brief, general statement of collection development philosophy, the document typically includes selection and de-selection criteria, a list of material formats that will be collected, a statement regarding donations, an overview of the depth and scope of the collection, and procedures for handling patron complaints about materials included in the collection. The American Library Association Library Bill of Rights is often included as an appendix to the document.

While librarians, then, are highly committed to collection development, the same cannot be said for many faculty. 'There are times when I'd be good at it [recommending books for purchase] and times when I wouldn't,' says **Ron White**. 'My being the one responsible for looking for books, that's just one more responsibility that takes me away from my research.' **Dan Mader,** a colleague who as department chair used to be responsible for recommending additions to the library collection, cites a similar concern. 'I've always thought it (collection development) was an important thing to do, but I don't miss doing it, because it takes some time to do it well.'

Mader's statement typifies the kind of dilemma many faculty feel in regard to collection development. Yes, it is an important duty, but there are many others that are more important. In a survey of the faculty at the College of Mount St. Joseph, Jenkins has shown that besides the obvious priorities of teaching and research, there are at least four peripheral duties they deem more important to the college than material selection: service on campus committees, advising, staying current in their field, and working on miscellaneous departmental duties as assigned by their chair (Jenkins, 1996: 20). Only performing community service and consulting were deemed less important. While this research was limited in scope to the faculty of one institution, it most likely serves as a barometer for all faculty. The results of the survey also indicate the importance of the academic collection development librarian. 'If faculty have so many more pressing duties to perform, the burden of selecting materials necessarily falls to the librarian' (Jenkins, 1996: 20).

Who should select?

Until the 1960s, material selection for the campus library was chiefly the responsibility of the faculty. At that time universities began employing subject bibliographers, largely as a result of the vast increases in book publication. On most smaller campuses, librarians began to assist their faculty colleagues in material selection only in the 1970s. As Fonfa points out, the assumption of these duties 'signified and impelled the professionalization of librarianship' (Fonfa, 1998: 35). With some notable exceptions, both groups largely seem to agree today that collection development is best done in tandem. Librarians must realize that faculty members do not have much time to devote to its practice and thus must find ways to make this responsibility as easy as possible. They must be realistic in their expectations. It is hard to imagine, for example, many faculty who would meet one librarian's qualifications for an ideal selector. According to Mary Duncan Carter, a professor should (1) know the currently productive scholars; (2) be thoroughly conversant with past scholarship; (3) know fully what the library has in his field; (4) know and make use of the sources of information for new materials; (5) be accurate in transcribing information about a title in requesting its purchase; (6) be broad in his interests; and, finally, (7) have a true knowledge of his students and remember the fact that he is selecting for them as well as for himself (Carter, 1974: 61).

Still, even some academic librarians have argued that selection should primarily be done by faculty. Dennis Dickinson, for example, leaves no doubt as to which group he feels is more qualified to select. He argues that material selection is 'more properly and more adequately done by faculty members than by librarians' (Dickinson, 1981: 138) because faculty possess superior knowledge of subject fields and are generally more effective, efficient, and economical in their selection. Central to his thesis is his assertion that 'American academics are overwhelmingly teachers rather than scholars' (142). Thus the materials they select are of real value to their students; they do not select only with their research projects in mind. In anticipation of a frequently voiced concern, Dickinson claims it is better to have sharply focused collections rather than the sort of bland collections which result when librarians select. He becomes positively sarcastic when he writes that arguments which contradict his

> appear to be based on no more than an unsupported and insupportable belief that librarians, for reasons unspecified, possess a magic power of transmutation which renders books over which they murmur cryptic incantations that are somehow more valuable than those not receiving their ministrations. (151)

Dickinson does admit that faculty selection has often been hampered by the group's general lack of commitment. To combat this problem, he proposes the establishment of a departmental liaison, a full-time faculty member who would serve as designated selector for his colleagues. In order to grant him enough time to do the job well, the designee would be freed of his other departmental duties.

In reviewing the literature on the topic, it seems that one major source of disagreement lies in whether one feels faculty or librarians best understand student needs, and whether or not this knowledge is more important than a knowledge of the curriculum and the library's role in supporting it. The curriculum is designed by the faculty for the student and the students' changing needs in great part determine the character of the curriculum. Both faculty and librarian serve the student, the former directly, the latter more indirectly. The faculty know how students *should* use the library, while librarians know how they *do* use the library.

Mark Sandler proposes a book selection plan that calls for an overall review of departmental allocations, followed by a prioritization of departmental needs, as determined by the library director. Meetings with each department's chair would produce collection development policies which, gathered together, would form the core of the library's general collection development document. 'By initiating a procedure that specifies the parameters of faculty responsibility for book selection, the library takes a long stride towards establishing the principle that it will exercise ultimate control over its collection' (Sandler, 1984: 71). One potential problem Sandler does not address is the difficulty the library director would face when attempting to thus prioritize the needs of each department. While he probably intends his plan for university libraries, on small college campuses it is not uncommon for departmental chairmanship to change every three years. Members of the faculty may not appreciate the stance Sandler takes toward them throughout his article. He thinks it may be necessary, for example, for librarians to train faculty in the selection of both current and retrospective materials. Furthermore, Sandler seems to believe that faculty are largely uninterested in student library needs and that they are less expert than simply credentialized.

Writing in 1985, Charles Gardner questioned the continued reliance of small college libraries on faculty to develop their collections.

> Continuity as well as professional responsibility obliges the library to assume selection leadership. It has become increasingly common for colleges to employ part-time and short-term teaching faculty. Continuity in collection building in such situations is very difficult unless the library provides it. Nor can part-time and transient faculty be expected to involve themselves in the ongoing

collection evaluation and preservation efforts so crucial to the maintenance of a strong, up-to-date undergraduate library. (144)

With the growth of OCLC and the advent of other networking arrangements in the mid-1980s, he correctly foresaw that 'common databases and networking mean new selection responsibilities that must be largely incumbent upon librarians' (144). While recognizing the role faculty will continue to play in material selection, Gardner advocates the 'abandonment of the departmental apportionment process' (145).

Ian Gordon is another advocate of librarian selectors. While acknowledging that many small academic libraries are forced to depend on faculty to select monographs, he calls on academic librarians in mid-sized and comprehensive universities to regain control of the book selection process. In 1999 he distributed a survey to librarians employed in Ontario, Canada's 17 largest universities. He found that 'librarians were solely responsible for the acquisition of monographic resources in only 30 per cent of all library systems' (Gordon, 2000: 688). Another 41 per cent collaborated with faculty in the process. It is the remaining 29 per cent to whom he makes his appeal. Why have they remained so passive? Comments from this group identify inertia, lack of time and energy, lack of support from library administrators, and wanting to avoid a potentially politically charged issue. Gordon contests this last point, if only through a vague assertion. 'Changing past practices need not be a political or difficult decision. Most faculty are willing to relinquish their responsibility if they are given an opportunity to remain active and equal participants' (689).

R.J. Dukes, then an associate professor of Physics at Charlestown College, makes a number of suggestions to facilitate better understanding between librarian and faculty member. He recommends that the library director should attend the occasional departmental meeting; that he should host an open house of sorts to improve communication; that he should provide instructions for book request forms and be ready to revise them as needed; and, finally, that he should do something about the faculty's ignorance of the library (Dukes, 1983). The article's conciliatory tone stems from the fact that it was originally an address Dukes gave to a library conference on acquisitions. The author freely admits that most of his faculty colleagues expect to have the final say regarding books in their field of expertise. Indeed, in the address/article he assumes that faculty will retain the major responsibility for selection. Still, any call to open the lines of communication between sometimes-feuding camps is welcome, and his appeal to librarians to educate faculty in the function and operation of the library is honest and flattering.

Daniel Gore, on the other hand, created a minor scandal with an article published in 1966 entitled 'The Mismanagement of College Libraries.' As the then head librarian at Macalester College, his purported purpose was to alert faculty members to a few problems in order to solicit their future cooperation. Instead, he managed to anger both them and his peers. In 1982 Gore revisited the issues first raised 16 years before and found that little progress had been made. He questions the value of the vast majority of faculty publications, books which he claims only serve to further clog libraries whose collections are becoming less and less accessible the larger they grow. He goes on to say that while librarians have shown a willingness and ability to change, faculty only advocate change from the lectern.

In 1986 Larry Hardesty conducted interviews with 40 faculty members from seven Indiana institutions. While local differences emerged, Hardesty was forced to conclude that faculty selectors in general lack a real understanding of what makes a book a good selection for an undergraduate library. He expressed concern that this deficiency might result in faculty-selected titles going largely unused by students. The previous year, Mary Sellen's study of faculty selectors at Pennsylvania State University indicated that while faculty viewed book selection as important, many 'expressed a need for more help in the selection process' (Sellen, 1985: 6). These findings, in turn, inspired Kuo to survey the faculty at Kean University to determine the extent to which faculty participated in book selection. Perhaps his most interesting finding was that junior faculty (those with 1–5 years of teaching experience) were more active selectors than their more seasoned colleagues. Kuo speculates that 'some junior faculty members are more active because they need more resources to build respectable status and enhance teaching' (Kuo, 2000: 30). Respondents showed that they understood the primary purpose of book selection for undergraduate libraries by choosing the 'good for students' option as the primary criterion for their selections.

Indeed, the question of who should select materials for academic libraries is not easy to answer. In her 1981 article 'Sources of Tension and Conflict Between Librarians and Faculty,' Mary Biggs concludes that 'it is true that a capable library administrator, advised by able subordinates, is in a better position to assess the broad needs of the academic community than any single faculty member could be' (186). Later in the same article, however, she concedes that 'building the collection can and should be defined as a basic faculty responsibility, as essential as meeting classes and producing articles' (196).

Commenting on the question of involving faculty in book selection, Ed Buis makes some sound points.

> Before condemning the sometimes impossible faculty demands for collection building and library services, librarians should review their own policies and procedures to see what sense they make outside the library. Often library policies appear sound in a room full of librarians, but once these policies hit the sunlight they have no validity whatsoever to non-library types such as university faculty. (Buis, 1993: 21)

Buis also notes how librarians can help faculty become better selectors. 'By assisting teaching faculty in defining departmental collection development goals and objectives, or collecting priorities for the department in support of those goals and objectives, librarians will see that their funds are placed where the greatest departmental needs exist' (23).

After all is said and done, however, studies have indicated that books selected by faculty members circulate at about the same rate as those selected by librarians. Connell, for example, studied two years of circulation data at the University of Illinois at Urbana-Champaign and found that although some differences between books selected by faculty or librarians do exist, 'the evidence is not conclusive that librarian-ordered materials circulate more often than do faculty-ordered materials' (Connell, 1991: 76). While Evans's (1970) research indicated that librarian-selected books were used more often, Bingham (1979) found exactly the opposite to be true. Vidor and Futas studied the question in 1988 but reached no certain conclusions. Geyer's (1977) study was equally inconclusive. It is also significant to note that most authors undertaking such studies were appalled at how many books – no matter who selected them – were never checked out.

Some have argued that good material selection 'is more dependent on the knowledge of publishing, bookselling, and the literature of disciplines than on the knowledge of subjects' (Ryland, 1982: 15). One might add to this list a knowledge of review sources, usually more readily available to librarians than faculty. For whichever group selects materials, their decisions should ideally be guided by published reviews of them. Resources such as *Booklist, Library Journal, Publisher's Weekly,* and, perhaps most importantly, *Choice* review hundreds of books each year for popular and academic markets.

Interestingly, Jenkins has demonstrated that on his campus at least, faculty often do not base their selection decision on reviews. His survey found that 88 per cent of librarian-initiated book recommendations stemmed from reviews. This finding made sense since 'book reviews have long been the trusted ally of collection development librarians' (Jenkins, 1999: 4). With their broad knowledge of their discipline, would faculty feel a similar reliance on published reviews? Specifically, faculty were asked to rate how important it is for them to have read a published review of a book before recommending it for library purchase. Thirty-seven per cent of respondents indicated that it was 'very important'; 28 per cent that it was 'important'; 28 per cent that it was 'important but not essential'; and 2 per cent that it was 'unimportant.' (Note that 5 per cent answered that they 'had never recommended books for library purchase.') In theory, then, reviews are nearly as important to faculty as they are to librarians. To calculate how true this was in practice, Jenkins tracked one year's book purchases. At first glance, the results of this study called into question the faculty survey responses. In actual practice, 61 per cent of faculty recommendations came from publishers' catalogs and only 39 per cent from review sources like *Choice*.

> Further investigation, however, revealed that more than half (57 per cent) of the non-reviewed requests stemmed from a single department, Religion. Omitting this department brought the percentages much closer to the survey results: 60 per cent reviewed, 40 per cent from catalogs. Appropriately, the Religion faculty all responded to the survey question that using reviews for selection was 'important, but not essential.' (Jenkins, 1999: 4–5)

Thus, 'while faculty recognize the potential importance of reviews, they are comfortable recommending a book without their benefit' (5).

Most faculty and librarians recognize that sharing responsibility for developing the collection makes the most sense. **Alan de Courcy**, for example, states:

> I would think a mix is best. It's hard for me to see how a librarian could know what are all the important journals in every field. So I think there would have to be consultation, with department faculty providing that kind of information. But the librarian has the

big picture, the needs of the library as a whole, and that's where their expertise has to come in.

His colleague, **Peg McPeak**, concurs.

I think a combination approach is best. Often you've done more research on a book. For example, you can say 'yes, but have you looked at this other title?' that is in a similar field. It needs to be a combination. Books and acquisitions – that's your profession.

The use of liaisons

No matter where material requests are generated, however, the library must retain the right to make final selection decisions. In small libraries, this power usually rests with the Head of Collection Development, or the Library Director. Many libraries designate departmental liaisons to conduct the initial phases of collection development. That is, library staff may be assigned one or more academic departments for which they have collection development responsibilities. This team approach can have some advantages over centralized collection development. It empowers staff members by involving them in the process; it exposes more librarians to the faculty; it distributes the workload so that no one is overwhelmed by the task; and, while following the general philosophy of the collection development policy, it lends a heterogeneous approach to developing the collection. Some liaisons embrace their duties enthusiastically, even going so far as to audit a course in their assigned department to get a true sense of student and faculty needs.

Yang has demonstrated that, on his campus (Texas A&M), faculty appreciate such liaison services. Not limited strictly to liaison's collection development responsibilities, his survey of the 64 faculty who serve as library representatives for their programs found that 75 per cent of them were 'pleased' with their library liaisons; 90 per cent ranked 'ordering books or serials for faculty' as 'very important'; 58 per cent of faculty surveyed responded that the library liaison's subject expertise or background did not affect the quality of services provided. It is important to note, however, that nearly 90 per cent of faculty in the College of Liberal Arts 'stressed that subject background was indispensable' (Yang, 2000: 127). As Neville and Williams have noted, the most useful liaison programs are those that continue to evolve and recognize the individual needs of separate academic departments. 'The nature of different disciplines mandates different buying strategies; the requirements of a mathematics collection and of a French literature collection differ so much that enforcing the same ordering procedures on both would be counterproductive' (1998: 525).

Of paramount importance to the use of liaisons is the disposition of the library staff. Some librarians do not want this task to be added to their regular responsibilities. In such cases, they will probably not give the job the time and attention it requires. Inconsistencies in procedure and philosophy sometimes creep into the team approach and end up outweighing any of its other advantages. Faculty may prefer working with only one librarian as well. It is always a good idea to keep all library procedures as simple as possible for them. A centralized approach ensures consistency, and selection decisions are informed by a knowledge of the entire collection, rather than just parts of it. In the end, whether or not to employ department liaisons will be based upon the willingness of the library staff, and the preference of the director, or collection development officer.

Allocation formulas

Another decision collection development librarians must make is whether to use allocation formulas. These are mathematical models designed to take the guesswork out of allocating departmental budgets. 'Allocation formulas operate on the basic premise that needs for objectivity and equity may be met by the quantification of a variety of numerical data' (Tuten, 1995: 1). In their 1989 article based on a survey of more than 800 academic libraries, Budd and Adams found that the following six variables (per academic discipline or department) were included most frequently in formulas: (1) number of students or credit hours; (2) cost of materials; (3) number of faculty; (4) circulation by department or subject area; (5) number of courses offered; and (6) number of student majors (1989). 'The wide range of considered elements only underscores the individuality of each formula' (Tuten, 1995: 2). David Schappert puts it well when he writes that the 'best formula is one that quantifies need with the minimum number of variables, since each variable adds to the time and expense of data collection, as well as the number of calculations that must be made to implement the formula' (1989: 141). Probably the hardest part of developing a good allocation formula is accurately gauging how the various elements should be weighed against each other. When budgetary times are good, faculty may pay little attention to allocation formulas. In leaner times, however, they will likely be more interested.

In his discussion of how to make allocation formulas appear fair to all participants, Schad writes that they need to agree on three things: (1) 'principles that guide allocation decisions; (2) measures that are used in applying those principles; and (3) principles that are followed' (Schad, 1987: 481). He suggests that *need, contributions*, and *equality* are reasonable principles upon which to base allocation decisions. The individual nature of an institution can help determine which principle is most appropriate, as well as which measures should be used. 'Colleges and universities seeking to foster the development and welfare of key departments will find the needs principle attractive' (481). Universities that value research may seek to measure factors such as a department's published research or the graduate credits it generates. Smaller institutions may prefer to use measures such as the circulation of library material in a department's discipline. The principle of contributions rewards academic departments that most clearly support their institution's mission. Finally, 'the principle of equality affords each recipient an equal share, regardless of differences in need or output' (481). While local factors make generalizing difficult, the contribution principle is usually judged fairest. Equally important to the philosophical approach chosen for allocation formulas, of course, is the consistent, accurate, correctable, and bias-free application of procedures used to determine each department's share of the budget. 'The appearance of fairness in the allocation process can be as important as actual fairness' (482–3).

Again, there are pros and cons to the use of allocation formulas. They can be a good way to explain to faculty how you arrived at the dollar allocation for their particular department. More arbitrary methods can make fund allocation more time-consuming and more difficult to justify. Then again, use of allocation formulas can be quite cumbersome and may result in skewed totals that do not make sense for your library. The Business department, for example, may win a major share of your allocation dollars according to the factors employed in the formula, but their need for books may be less than that of other departments. While the English department may not have many majors per year, students in their so-called support courses will need to use a great number of library books to complete their assignments. Interdisciplinary courses may also get the short shrift using formulas. In short, allocation formulas attempt to make this most difficult of decisions a science rather than an art. They can be useful in establishing a base figure (which can then be artistically adjusted), but I have yet to encounter a formula that I would want to use as an oracle. There are too many immeasurable factors that must be considered in the equation to make them a truly useful tool.

A related topic is whether or not to inform faculty how much money has been allocated (in whatever way) for purchase of materials to support their department's courses. If you do let them know, you run the risk that they will begin comparing their figure to that assigned to their colleagues. (Chances are good that they will share this information if the topic of the library comes up.) You will then have to defend your decisions. Some librarians prefer not to inform their faculty so that they don't recommend items simply to meet their departmental quota. Those who subscribe to this school of thought simply base their allocation on the number of requests they receive from faculty. This approach can be dangerous, though, too, since a figure isn't always known in the planning stages of the fiscal year. A good rule is to determine if the system in place is working to both your and the faculty's satisfaction. If it is, why rock the boat? If it isn't, consider experimenting for a year with another approach.

Allocation formulas are used to a lesser extent with periodical or non-print budgets. Periodical subscriptions imply an annual commitment and are recommended in far smaller numbers than books. Non-print materials, while highly prized by faculty since they often figure directly in lesson plans, are also usually recommended on a less regular basis than books.

Approval plans

'Conventional wisdom would have one believe that approval plans are appropriate only for large academic libraries. According to this outdated notion, small college libraries have neither the funds nor the staff to make this more impersonal style of collection development effective at their institutions' (Jenkins, 2003: 179). It has been my experience, however, that approval plans identify recent publications in certain disciplines not adequately covered by traditional book review sources such as *Choice* or *Booklist*. Establishing approval plan profiles is not terribly difficult or time-consuming. Vendor staff are quite helpful and attentive to an institution's individual needs. They can help you decide if you should receive books that fit your profile, or simply slips (either in print, or electronically) that identify such titles. It is also important to involve appropriate faculty members in the creation of a profile. Yang, for example, found that 85 per cent of faculty who responded to his survey at Texas A&M 'expressed an interest in being involved in reviewing the library's approval plan' (Yang, 2000: 127). Once you have developed a draft profile, invite them to look at it and make suggestions.

Subject parameters for your profile can be as general as Religion, or as specific as Zoroastrianism. Non-subject parameters to establish for your profile include the following: imprint date, binding (cloth, paper, loose-leaf, etc.), format (collected works, field guides, textbooks, etc.), language, content level (general academic, advanced academic, etc.), new editions, non-book formats, place of publication, price ceiling, size, and geographic specifications (US, world, Pacific Rim, etc.).

At the College of Mount St. Joseph, the approval plan has been quite effective. When we disseminated slips to our Education faculty, for example, they responded favorably. In fact, the number of titles ordered for this discipline rose from 86 in fiscal year 1999–2000 to 133 in fiscal year 2000–01 the first year we implemented the approval plan. Results in the three other disciplines we chose for our profile were similarly encouraging, as shown in the Table 2.1.

Table 2.1   Titles ordered by discipline

Discipline	Fiscal year 1999–2000	Fiscal year 2000–01
Education	86	133 titles ordered
Nursing	36	87
Physical therapy	33	49
Pastoral/family studies	11	51
Total	166	320

'Thus, we were able to nearly double our purchases in these four important areas of the curriculum. Even in disciplines where faculty participation in collection development is minimal, slips can help library selectors keep these areas current' (Jenkins, 2003: 180).

Very briefly, one less traditional method of collection development that some schools have begun to practise is accompanying faculty to large local bookstores and letting them choose titles off the shelf. Faculty sometimes bring students along for such outings. Since most large bookstores have liberal return policies, duplicate purchases present no real problem. I have found this practice especially effective in developing our collection of music CDs. Aside from the obvious enjoyment such trips bring, librarians benefit by discussing selection techniques while faculty benefit by building 'their part of the collection to augment courses they are or will be teaching' (Brantz, 2002: 264). Additionally, one should never underestimate the effect such immediate gratification has on participants. While evidence is only anecdotal, circulation of items purchased in this manner seems higher than those bought in more conventional ways.

Cooperative collection development

'Perhaps the most important development for libraries during the current decade has been the move from organizational self-sufficiency to a col-laborative survival mode as personified by the growth of library con-sortia. Information technology is now enabling a level of cooperation that is much broader and deeper than ever before' (Allen and Hirshon, 1998: 36). Consortia of various sizes and purposes exist in all 50 American states and across the world. Due to cooperative lending agreements, collection development librarians must now think in terms of selecting materials not simply for their own libraries, but also for those of their fellow consortium members.

One of the most difficult factors to weigh in making such decisions is determining if an item is already held by a sufficient number of members of your consortium. Admittedly, this figure is quite difficult to establish. Oberlin College's response to the issue is reflected in their document titled 'Purchasing Monographs in View of OhioLINK.' Their rationale is well stated.

> Since OhioLINK markedly improves access to library resources statewide, it offers an opportunity to rethink how we select books for the library collection. The library's acquisitions budget can be used most effectively if selectors carefully consider when books

should be purchased for the collections and when it is sufficient for titles to be accessible through OhioLINK. The opportunity to rely on OhioLINK for some materials that would have been purchased in the past allows us to consider for purchase materials that are less widely available, thereby providing access to a richer and more diverse collection of materials for Oberlin's library users and those within the OhioLINK consortium. (Carpenter, 1997)

Thus faculty selectors at Oberlin are asked to designate book requests as Local, Accessible, or Desirable. Local is defined as books that 'need to be locally owned.' These include books 'needed for frequent or prolonged use to support undergraduate teaching and learning, and important books in disciplines taught at Oberlin needed to insure the integrity of the library's collections.' Accessible is defined as books 'that must be readily accessible, either through OhioLINK or through purchase for Oberlin's library collections.' Examples include 'specialized scholarly treatises primarily needed for research, books needed infrequently or for brief periods, and books of lesser disciplinary importance.' Desirable is defined as 'books that would be desirable to have readily accessible – either through OhioLINK or through purchase for Oberlin's library collections.' Examples include 'significant books relevant to Oberlin's teaching and research interests that are not readily accessible on OhioLINK.' Such policies will grow in importance as more and more libraries join consortia.

Faculty members I've worked with indicate a willingness to embrace similar philosophies. **Dan Mader** notes that

> OhioLINK is wonderful. It is wonderful to know that when you need a book you can get it within three to five days. When I was an undergraduate, interlibrary loan took two or three weeks, and by the time you got the book it might be too late. You see Ohio-LINK as just a greater library. I think it probably does affect the intensity I feel about owning a book for our local collection. I would feel more intensely about it if I wanted to have the book readily available to show students in a studio class, or if I wanted to put it on reserve.

Alan de Courcy:

> Having this kind of access through OhioLINK is incredible, especially at a small institution like ours. There are things like videos that I still feel it's important for us to get here, but it

doesn't make sense to me that we try to build up a big collection of books any more. I find that OhioLINK works wonderfully well.

Another factor in cooperative collection development that cannot be ignored is the stagnation or reduction of material budgets. Since the days of the Farmington Plan (established in 1942), librarians have chased the holy grail of cooperative collection development with little success. This ambitious plan fell into disuse in the early 1970s, thanks in part to reductions in materials budgets, poor administration, and growing confusion as to its actual mission (Gaines, 1994: 193). The combination of low material budgets for individual members and excessive duplication of titles in the OhioLINK consortium central catalog led Jenkins to initiate an approval-plan-based cooperative collection development project.

> Dubbed SWORCS (Southwestern Ohio Religious Cooperative), the plan experienced a lengthy gestation period, and we have encountered some of the same difficulties which doomed the Farmington Plan. The germ of the idea sprang from a comment heard at an OhioLINK committee meeting that the consortium's subject groups (Art, Biology, etc.) should be more actively promoting cooperative collection development. Instead of continuing unnecessary duplication of titles in subject areas, why not purchase titles outside the core held by few or no consortium members? Since my institution is one of four in the immediate Cincinnati area with a religious affiliation, I sensed an opportunity. Could librarians from a small group of religious institutions attempt a cooperative collection development project in the field of religious studies which might serve as a model for later statewide application? (Jenkins, 2004: 130)

Though still immature, the SWORCS project has proven feasible. Participating institutions have begun spending a minimum of $500 a year to purchase titles about religions outside the Judeo-Christian tradition (Confucianism, Sikhism, Taoism, Shinto, Jainism, Bahai, Zoroastrianism, Rastafarianism, Tenrikyo, and various African religions). It seems clear that cooperative collection development in any discipline will succeed only in areas like these which are peripheral to the core. Such a concentration also makes faculty buy-in to such projects more probable. As long as budget commitments remain low, and as long as they are consulted, faculty are unlikely to raise any serious objections to such librarian-initiated projects.

Weeding

Just as important as deciding which materials to add to your collection is deciding which should be removed. Weeding or deselection guidelines should be included in your library's collection development policy. Criteria for removing material from the collection typically include: date of item's publication, its physical condition, its relevance to the current curriculum, its circulation record, whether new editions have been published, whether it is included in standard bibliographies or lists of best books (such as *Books for College Libraries*), and number of available copies both in your local collection and in any relevant consortial collections. Certain disciplines need to be weeded more often than others. Collections in fields such as Nursing, Computer Science, Health Sciences, and Business, for example, will need to be examined more often than disciplines whose works are more timeless: Art, Literature, History, and Religion.

It is just as important to include faculty in this process as it is to handle their requests for the addition of new materials. A method I have found effective and simple is to place paper flags in books which meet your deselection criteria and then invite faculty to look these over and remove flags from titles they believe should be retained. This system makes the process relatively painless and reassures faculty that you regard them as partners in collection management.

Woeful tales of journal cancellation projects are all too common in library literature. Faculty – especially in the Natural Sciences and Social Sciences – often feel more strongly about journal titles than they do about individual books. Simply deciding how long to retain runs of journal titles, while difficult, is less likely to draw faculty ire. Since shelf space in smaller libraries is often at a premium, and since the demands of undergraduate research are less intense than those for graduate studies undertaken at large universities, it is sometimes necessary to restrict runs of journal titles to periods of 10–30 years. Again, the discipline involved usually influences such decisions. Faculty in professional fields such as Business, Nursing, and Education may be content with the library retaining only the current ten years of their journals. Faculty in most other fields will be more comfortable knowing that the current twenty or thirty years of their key journals are available both for them and their undergraduate students. If their program is accredited by a national body or association, they will know the group's guidelines for journal retention. In short, in this, and all other collection development issues, communicating with your faculty is paramount. As Felix Chu observes, 'the library can be a proactive force if the faculty trust the librarians to make appropriate choices and the librarians trust the faculty to watch out for institutional well-being' (1997: 17).

Conclusions

Working with faculty to develop the library's collection raises a number of questions. How much should librarians rely on faculty to request materials? Will they have enough time to do this work effectively? Do staff librarians have interest in working as liaisons with academic departments? Should allocation formulas be used to determine how to divide the materials budget? Do existing formulas meet the library's needs, or must a hybrid be developed? Will using an approval plan free up staff time yet also identify appropriate titles to add? Answers to these questions will, of course, vary greatly from library to library depending on both the philosophy of the director and his knowledge of the faculty members with whom he works. Librarians must recognize that while faculty should always be consulted regarding collection development decisions, they cannot always be depended on to participate actively in the process. As John Gay reminds us, 'There is no dependence that can be sure but a dependence upon one's self.'

3

Working with faculty in information literacy and other public services

'Information is the currency of democracy.' – Thomas Jefferson

Teaching students and faculty to more effectively use the library and its services and resources has long been central to the mission of the academic library. First called simply 'library orientation' or 'library use instruction,' the practice began to be known as 'bibliographic instruction' in the 1970s. Perhaps its most successful proponent was Evan Farber, who was Library Director at Earlham College (Richmond, Indiana) for more than thirty years. In an article published in 1995, the now-retired Farber states that while he witnessed numerous technological changes in his career, a number of factors influencing bibliographic instruction have remained constant. Chief among these are the necessity to work with faculty to design effective instruction and the accompanying realization that not all faculty are cooperative. Successful in his efforts to involve most faculty with library-based assignments in bibliographic instruction, Farber did encounter some dissenters. These he characterized as

> people who thought they could not spare the time either to talk about instruction or to implement it were territorial – that is, reluctant to share their classes with anyone; were mostly taught the way *they* were taught; had fragile egos so that it was risky to criticize their library assignments or even to make suggestions; and they could not think of librarians as peers with whom they could share their students. (1995: 431–2)

At the same time, Farber does concede that, over time, faculty have become 'more open' and 'less defensive.' More significantly, he notes that 'because library technology has changed things so much since many of these faculty were in graduate school, they know that librarians can find information they cannot; in a sense, they have gained a new respect for librarians' (432).

Tim Lynch agrees:

> It's getting increasingly important to have a good relationship (with campus librarians) because the tools by which students gather information are changing so quickly. When I started my graduate education it was still sitting on those bar stools in the library with card catalog drawers, writing down call numbers. Just going to the computerized catalog was a huge step, and that was just doing the same thing a different way. Now with all the search engines, the full-text has changed everything. My way of approaching my research has changed. If you don't have a good relationship with librarians, or if you don't put your students in contact with librarians to learn the tools then they will never learn them.

Perhaps then it is not surprising that in recent years Information Literacy (IL) has become *the* hot topic in the world of academic librarianship. Witness the dozens of presentations on the subject at any academic library conference; witness the hundreds of articles on the topic in library literature; witness its presence on virtually every academic library's website. One can only surmise that the recent proliferation of electronic library resources and the rapidity with which they seem to change has left academic librarians anxious about the ability of their users to make the best possible use of these tools. As of 2004, the Google search engine alone reported that it indexes more than four million sites. With the growth of library consortia resulting in continually cheaper access to databases, it is not unusual for even a small academic library to offer more than one hundred of them. Add to this the fact that books continue to be published in record numbers, and one gets some idea of the volume of information that awaits undergraduates.

Mary Kay Fleming describes the pernicious effect such superfluity of information has had on the academic habits of her contemporary college students.

> The majority of students have no concept of the difference between refereed and non-refereed publications, or between the

Internet and the library. And that is really disturbing at this level. The other thing that we're all facing is that students are coming into college with significant experience with the Internet from grade school and high school. That's where the bad habits start. I think they get bad habits in not recognizing the difference between quality and non-quality sources, and I think that they learn to be careless about copyright. Nobody's saying, 'You have to reword this, it's not okay to do this.' The concept of intellectual property with writing is hard to understand. Students now think that they have all the same resources of a library at their command over a computer. They're picking up a lot of garbage and acting like it's equivalent to journal articles.

In short, today's students 'have grown up in a world where fast is good and instant is better' (Burkhardt, MacDonald and Rathemacher, 2003: ix). In their highly influential book, *Millennials Rising: The Next Great Generation*, Neil Howe and William Strauss define millennials as those born in 1982 or after. According to their study of this generation, millennials are, in a nutshell, optimists, enjoy working collaboratively, happily follow rules, enjoy school, and 'believe in the future and see themselves as its cutting edge' (2000: 10). In their pre-college education, they have been assigned more homework than their predecessors, worked longer hours to complete it, and felt more stress about eventual college admission. 'They prefer those subjects in which they and the world can measure their objective progress' (161). More advice on how to best communicate with millennials in a library context comes from Lori Ricigliano. She reminds us to 'limit the number of points in a session by covering a few basic concepts' (2001: 124); 'show you care' by reaching out to students as individuals; vary your presentations to include graphics; keep your presentations as short as possible; 'make it fun' and 'show you have a sense of humor'; allow for frequent feedback; and 'focus on end results' (125). It is always good to remember that students 'want to know why they must learn something before they take an active interest in learning a new skill' (126).

ALA information literacy survey

The results of a 2001 survey conducted by ALA highlight the prominence of information literacy in higher education today. Updating similar information first gathered in 1997, 710 institutions (26 per cent of those contacted) of various sizes responded. Private colleges, community colleges, and comprehensive universities each accounted for a quarter of respondents, with the remaining quarter made up of four-year public universities (9 per cent) and those designated as 'research and doctoral' (16 per cent). 'The survey results show that a fairly uniform set of standards for information literacy are widely accepted by higher education institutions of all types' (Sonntag, 2001: 998). Only 123 (17 per cent) responded, however, that they had adopted specific information literacy *requirements*.

One question asked which groups were responsible for implementing information literacy standards. Of those institutions that had, in fact, adopted such standards (27 per cent), 42 per cent indicated that 'Librarians and library committees exclusively' were responsible for standards implementation; 15 per cent left this work to their 'General Education Committees'; another 12 per cent to their 'Information Literacy or Information Technology/Computing Groups.' The remaining responses were divided among curriculum committees, specific departments, academic senates, assessment groups, and the like. Another question asked how institutions are conducting information literacy. Most institutions appear to be using more than one method; 'infusing' information literacy into the curriculum was the most popular answer, followed by using 'computer instruction,' or 'integrating' IL into the curriculum. Making IL part of the General Education Requirements was the least popular method of passing it along to students. Respondents indicated that mastery of IL is being measured via the following methods: pre- and post-tests, completion of a specific IL course, completion of in-class assignments, or via online workbooks.

As an aside, it's worth mentioning that literacy in emerging technology is more linked to information literacy than many think. Simply because they grew up with the technology available to them does not mean that all of today's students have the time or ability to keep up with its continued progress. While Davis's (1997) study found that 83 per cent of employers believe that 'computer competency skills' are 'important' or 'very important' in hiring decisions, when asked about the abilities and training of recent college graduates, human resource executives mentioned a lack of computer literacy skills as one of their weaknesses (Thompson, 1992: 23). Meanwhile, high school students continue to believe that a sound technical education is 'their single best ticket to better jobs and better pay' (*Vocational Training News*, 2003: 6). Indeed, like their library peers, instructional technology specialists on college and university campuses are struggling to define and implement standards of technological or computer literacy.

Nearly all educational institutions, then, recognize a need to help their students learn how to use technology and information effectively. Still, some areas of concern emerged in the 'comments' sections of the 2001 ALA survey. Respondents indicated that some faculty view IL skills as remedial. Other institutions support IL in theory, but are unwilling to mandate standards for it. Finally, the familiar lament over lack of time is heard. Faculty acknowledge its importance, but simply have no time to devote to it. When interpreting these results, it is important to recognize how recent a phenomenon the topic (at least as named 'information literacy') is: 48 per cent of respondents indicated that their programs had existed three years or fewer. Perhaps the most positive spin to put on the survey was expressed by one respondent who wrote 'Faculty are now aware of what librarians can teach and how it relates to what faculty teach.'

Can librarians rely on faculty to teach IL skills?

Historically, faculty have shown that while they support the idea of library instruction in principle, they do not always follow through once specifics need to be planned. Hardesty has speculated that aspects of 'faculty culture' are to blame for this disconnect. While acknowledging that 'some violence is done to the individual in concentrating on the multitude' (1995: 345), he cites the following aspects of faculty culture that hinder their embracement of library instruction: 'a feeling of lack of time; emphasis on content, professional autonomy, and academic freedom; de-emphasis on the applied and the process of learning; and resistance to change' (356). This first concern – lack of time – has served as something of a refrain for this book. 'Teaching – good teaching – requires lots of time, and we just can't expect BI [bibliographic instruction] to be the major concern of a good teacher' (Farber, 1992: 4). Writing in 1999, Hardesty still is forced to conclude that 'the library will become central to the educational mission of an institution only if someone is trying aggressively to put it there' (246).

This someone, of course, is the academic librarian. He must take the initiative with faculty and make their participation in IL as time efficient as possible. The other concerns cited above, while important, play smaller roles in resistance to adopting IL and, more importantly, are much more difficult to address. It is essential that faculty members never feel as if librarians are telling them how to teach, or what to emphasize in their courses. Great tact and considerable rhetorical skills must be used to convince skeptical faculty members of IL's value. Rather than continually tilting at such windmills, I would advise concentrating at first on those more open to conversion. When enough faculty become convinced of IL's merits, word of mouth will spread the good news. Faculty are much more likely to be convinced by fellow faculty than by librarians.

Definitions of information literacy

In the face of recent emphasis on Information Literacy, some librarians have asked 'haven't we been doing this – library instruction – all along?' Wilson provides some useful distinctions. She identifies four terms librarians have used for instruction over the years. '*Library orientation* comprises service activities designed to welcome and introduce users and potential users to services, collections, building layouts, and the organization of materials' (1995: 154). Obviously, this is the least ambitious method and can often be done by staff or even students. '*Library instruction* refers to instruction in the use of libraries, with an emphasis on institution-specific procedures, collections, and policies' (155). Such sessions are now often presented electronically and constitute the next-highest level of instruction. 'In contrast to library instruction, *bibliographic instruction* goes beyond the physical boundaries of the library and beyond institution-specific confines' (156). This term implies a greater emphasis on the teaching aspect of the librarian's job. The final term Wilson employs, *information management education*, sounds very similar to our current notion of information literacy. It 'refers to instructing users in the identification, retrieval, evaluation, and use of information' (156). Lori Arp notes that by substituting the word 'literacy' for 'instruction,' librarians signal a definite change in purpose, one which they may not realize, and may not want to retain. Information literacy, she argues, 'has a product – an information literate individual' (1990: 46). This individual's skills must be assessed in order to provide validity to the term 'literate.' Are librarians prepared for this greater task? 'Bibliographic instruction, on the other hand, is a methodology, some would argue a discipline, which enables skills and concepts to be learned' (46). To sidestep this distinction, she proposes a less ambitious term for what librarians currently provide: 'information literacy instruction.'

Whatever you call it, the basic idea remains to educate the library user. Farber points out, for example, that

> in the pre-electronic era, students typically thought that if they found any books or articles on their topics in the library, they were worth using. It was difficult enough to teach them that not everything in print was valid, and that there are criteria, intellectual filters one can use to separate the wheat from the chaff, the scholarly from the spurious. (1999: 232)

Perhaps one can say that where Information Literacy differs a bit from its predecessors is in its *added* emphasis on evaluation and use of information. According to the American Library Association (ALA), 'to be information literate, a person must be able to recognize when information is needed and have the ability to locate, evaluate, and use effectively the needed information' (available online at: *http://www .ala.org/ala/acrl/acrlpubs/whitepapers/presidential.htm*).

Shapiro and Hughes suggest additional detail to ALA's definition of IL. They believe that

> information literacy should in fact be conceived more broadly as a new liberal art that extends from knowing how to use computers and access information to critical reflection on the nature of information itself, its technical infrastructure, and its social, cultural and even philosophical context and impact – as essential to the mental framework of the educated information-age citizen as the trivium of basic liberal arts (grammar, logic, and rhetoric) was to the educated person in medieval society. (1996: 3/6)

More useful is their division of IL into seven dimensions, succinctly defined in an article by Cunningham and Lanning in the following manner: (1) tool literacy – 'ability to use print/electronic resources and software'; (2) resource literacy – 'ability to understand the form, format, location and access methods of information resources'; (3) social-structural literacy – 'knowledge of how information is socially situated and produced, including the process of scholarly publication'; (4) research literacy – 'ability to understand and use information technology tools to conduct research, including discipline-related software'; (5) publishing literacy – 'ability to produce a text/multimedia report of research results'; (6) emerging technology literacy – 'ability to adapt to, understand, evaluate, and use continually emerging innovations in information technology'; and, finally, (7) critical literacy – 'ability to evaluate information technologies critically in terms of their intellectual, human, and social strengths and weaknesses as well as their potentials and limits, benefits and costs' (Cunningham and Lanning, 2002: 344).

While attainment of all seven of these skills lies beyond the scope of most undergraduates, the expanded definition does provide a number of jumping-off points. Certainly faculty would appreciate their students gaining a better understanding of research literacy. For example, **Rick Sparks** believes that his students at both the undergraduate and graduate level

> dislike the research process intensely. They don't like to do a research project. They do it because they have to, not because they want to. I collaborate with the librarians by asking them to walk them through and show them how to do a literature search. The students who take the research process seriously find that very helpful.

His colleague, **Alan de Courcy** concurs.

> Our graduate students need almost as much help with their research skills as our undergraduates. The lack of research skills across the board is appalling. I don't see students getting enough help in learning how to research in the classroom from their regular teachers. I think the need to learn how to do research is more important than ever because they have access to so much information.

Too often, faculty think of the library as only a collection of books and journals, and not as a resource organized and managed by librarians. **Jim Bodle** is one faculty member who understands this distinction and values the instructional services librarians can provide.

> I think that a lot of faculty – and I'm speaking a little more broadly than just our campus – just think that you send students off someplace and that some magical librarian will solve all their problems. One of the biggest stumbling blocks is that it's impor-

tant to know who the librarian is. You need to be able to tell students in very specific ways how to access the library because students for about the last five years or so have known less and less about any library. It seems to me that some students don't even know that there is a library. They think that nothing exists if it's not on the Internet.

The faculty's attitude towards using the library is vital. **Dan Mader** recognizes this:

> If they don't use it [the library] enough it's our fault as teachers. Over the past five years we've been told that the Internet can do everything, but as teachers we need to make clear that the Internet is not the library, that there are things in books that won't be on the Internet. We have to give assignments that make students go into the library.

One of his colleagues, **Sue Johnson**, notes the importance of faculty modeling good library use. 'Sometimes I think faculty don't use the library enough. We're not over here enough unless we're working on a particular project. One time I walked over here to get something and saw one of my students. She said, "what are you doing here?"'

Librarians' attitudes towards faculty

If many faculty appreciate what librarians can do for their students, too many librarians bring negative attitudes towards faculty to their IL efforts. As part of their seven-year (1995–2002) study of the major IL listserv (first called BI-L and later changed to ILI-L), Julien and Given found that while librarians characterized themselves as 'dedicated, caring individuals, who continually strive to meet students' needs' (2002: 77), they sometimes found faculty lazy or 'uncaring.' Other findings echo some of the problems discussed earlier in this book. Librarians found faculty 'possessive' about class time and their students, 'territorial,' and 'inflexible.'

> Such deliberate, moral positioning was very common in postings concerning faculty members' personal attitudes and behaviors. Teaching faculty were variously described as having high opinions of themselves, as being rude, 'touchy,' rarely cooperative,

recalcitrant about change, and out of touch with their students' skill levels. (77)

Apparently, many librarians used the list to warn others of potential problems they might face from faculty.

Various posters suggested that librarians should expect 'trouble' from teaching faculty, that some faculty have 'inappropriate' or 'bad' attitudes, that librarians should expect their requests to be ignored (or 'blown off'), and that some faculty need to be 'frightened' into 'compliance' (by pointing out that familiar library resources are changing or being eliminated). Listserv subscribers were warned not to let themselves be 'pushed around' by faculty, so as not to drain librarians' 'emotional survival bank.' Some posters noted that teaching faculty need to be 'tricked' into paying attention to the library, by being cajoled with food and low-pressure environment. (78)

Other postings questioned faculty members' ability to gain new skills or accurately inform their students as to what resources the library offers. 'Faculty also were berated for not understanding the difference between the "internet" and web-based academic resources, as well as for crafting inappropriate or generally "poor" assignments for their students' (79). Positive comments about faculty were few and far between.

Such bitterness can only perpetuate the problems librarians and faculty have experienced in their common mission to educate students. I can only concur with Julien and Given's conclusion:

The images of troublesome, arrogant faculty, who have little understanding of librarians' roles, point to a problem at the core of the relationship issue; that until librarians embrace faculty as clients themselves, deserving of the same level of respect and support afforded undergraduate and graduate students, IL librarians may continue to fight an uphill battle to bring faculty members onside. (2002: 82–3)

Information literacy methods

If and when faculty become convinced of the importance of information literacy, what are the methods most often used? Librarians have generally used print handouts, lectures and tours of the faculty, lectures in the instructor's classroom, and, finally, entire courses devoted to learning how to find, use, and evaluate information. Let us examine for a moment the merits and weaknesses of each of these methods. 'Written library guides' of the past are beginning to be replaced by web pages designed by librarians to meet various instructional needs. Such pages have proved quite popular with faculty since they can assign their students to make use of them outside of class. 'Seat time' is very precious to faculty and they are often loath to give it up even for one class period for library instruction. The use of web-based instruction sometimes convinces reluctant faculty members to participate when they otherwise wouldn't. Librarians' time is also precious, of course, and the major disadvantage of instructional web pages is that they can be very time-consuming to create and maintain.

Patrick Ragains outlines the process of instructional web page design in an article published in *Research Strategies*. He believes that common components of each page should include: (1) 'links to key points on the library Web site, including the library home page, the online catalog, a page of reference information, electronic journals, and a link back to the list of subject pages'; (2) 'a subject-related list of proprietary online in dexes and databases'; and (3) 'recommended subject-related Web sites that are freely available' (2001: 86). Other useful links to include are those to interlibrary loan request forms and information on how to access library resources from off-campus. In order to save time and create consistency, Ragains suggests preparing a template that can be modified for specific needs.

The second method, lectures and tours, requires that you somehow capture the attention of the students. As one librarian notes, this is not easy. They 'are a hardened lot, sophisticated yet ignorant, cynical yet strangely naïve. Most of them have little enthusiasm for a lecture or demonstration on the use of library resources' (McKinzie, 1997: 19). A dry, passive, scripted talk is doomed to failure. Librarians must try to make such presentations as spontaneous as possible and pepper them with questions that demand student involvement. Solicit from them possible topics for their research. If they know you are going to help them save time in the long run, they will listen more attentively. Encourage the faculty to attend these sessions and to actively participate.

> Faculty comments – off-hand and casual though they may be – can increase an instruction's effectiveness remarkably. My advice to librarians is that you make sure that your teaching colleagues

with whom you work really know this. If those faculty have a real sense of their value as part of a demonstration or a discussion of information resources, they won't schedule your visit to their class or plan their class's visit to the library when they intend to attend a scholarly conference. (20)

Due to the advent of the web and the proliferation of electronic resources, presentations given by librarians in an instructor's classroom are more likely to succeed than was previously the case. Many classrooms now are equipped with projecting PCs which allow librarians to conduct virtual tours of the library. Some advantages this approach enjoys over others are that sufficient seating is guaranteed, the instructor is more often present, students are probably more likely to respond to questions in their familiar classroom setting, and the message that remote use of the library is not only possible but productive is driven home loud and clear.

Many librarians insist that it is only possible to do justice to IL by devoting an entire course to the topic. At the Mount we used this method for years with success, teaching a course called Information Retrieval as adjuncts of the Business department (which included Computer Information Systems courses). The class met once a week for the entire 15 week semester and covered practical library research skills for course-related needs, methods and techniques of searching various databases, the use of reference materials and periodicals, and how to take maximum advantage of the World Wide Web as a research tool. As a capstone to the course, students were required to create an annotated bibliography on a topic of their choosing based on these elements. The one-credit course was one of five possible ways to meet the three-credit computer literacy requirement then in place (the others being one-credit courses in word processing, spreadsheets, databases, and SPSS). One research-intensive program (Physical Therapy) even required their students to take it. When the computer literacy requirement was abolished as part of a major curriculum revision, however, so was the course. At least one Mount faculty member, **Sue Johnson** of the Nursing department, laments its passing. 'I wish the library would offer an Informatics course,' she says. She believes only half of the junior-level students in her classes are information literate. While a number of such courses exist around the country today, it can be very difficult to establish their place in the curriculum. Faculty co-sponsorship is usually necessary.

If Davis's (1999) study of 'eight methods for learning computer literacy skills' is at all comparable to how students learn information literacy skills, however, librarians may need to rethink their approaches to the topic. 'Trial and Error, Credit Classes, and Peer Support were clearly ranked as being more effective than Faculty Support, Online Help, Printed Documentation, Non-Credit Workshops, or Drop-In Clinics' (70). In follow-up focus groups, Davis gleaned that students largely preferred to operate in 'learn as needed' mode.

> There was unanimous agreement that professors assume students to have specific software skills without providing any support or training. This was a source of considerable frustration and stress for many students. On the other hand, students do not want professors to spend significant amounts of their time teaching software instead of course content. (71)

It seems fair to assume that substituting 'computer literacy skills' for 'specific software skills' in the sentence above would not change the veracity of the statement. Discussions also indicated that students enjoy working in groups and that this is an effective way to approach most any skill that must be learned. Any librarian with reference desk experience can verify this. If at all possible, students want to learn from their peers.

Librarians at Virginia Polytechnic and State University (Virginia Tech) have developed a grant-funded peer advising (PA) IL program called One2One. Peer advisers, they argue, can spend more time helping patrons than Reference staff, free reference staff from answering repetitive questions, and create patrons who ask better questions at the Reference Desk than would otherwise be the case (Auer, Seamans and Pelletier, 2003: 26). Training for such students is, of course, extensive and time-consuming. Sessions were created for 'topic focusing, resource selection, and database and online catalog searching' (27). To help monitor the program's success, PAs were asked to describe their experiences each day via journal entries. Because fully half of the One2One sessions are scheduled in advance, PAs have time to bone up on the topic at hand. Students seeking assistance are cautioned that their PA will not be doing their assignment for them. While the authors admit that they should have emphasized to the PAs more 'the crucial skill of knowing when to refer to reference librarians' (27), the program has proved successful. Equally effective has been a similar approach at the University of Massachusetts-Dartmouth. Here, library 'interns' lend individual library research assistance to students in large classes. The program is advertised on campus by flyers and word-of-mouth, and the Writing & Reading Center may also refer students to it. Though assessment survey data is scant, the thirty-minute sessions seem to be popular with students and indicate that 'with good training, undergraduates can ably assist other students in basic library research tasks' (Lindsay, 2000: 15).

Smith presents another interesting alternative approach to teaching IL. It is faculty, she believes, not librarians who are best suited to teach their students information literacy skills. 'Integrating information literacy throughout the undergraduate curriculum is limited as long as librarians insist on doing the instruction themselves' (Smith, 1997: abstract). Employed at an institution that includes only three professional librarians, she suggests that many library staffs are not large enough to do the job effectively.

> Our efforts to teach students have undermined our ability to integrate information literacy throughout the curriculum by using up time and energy that would be better focused on institution-wide initiatives that lead to shared educational goals and objectives throughout the campus. (1/7)

The number of faculty at institutions like hers, Smith argues, is small enough to target and teach. 'Information literacy will be integrated throughout the curriculum only if faculty recognize its importance, make it a goal as they develop their syllabi, and know how to teach information literacy themselves' (3/7). They are the only group powerful enough on campus to make IL part of the curricular core, but they must first be educated by librarians as to IL's importance. The author suggests sharing published IL competencies with faculty at meetings and workshops, especially during orientation in the fall. Librarians serving on campus committees should relentlessly stress IL's importance. Finally, 'information literacy will be integrated throughout the curriculum only if librarians responsible for instruction commit their time primarily to faculty development and collaboration' (5/7).

Nancy Niles describes a similar approach used at SUNY (State University of New York) Cobleskill. In 1996, the library 'discontinued the BI program and has since attempted to direct our instructional efforts toward preparing faculty to incorporate information literacy skills within their own classes – a teach the teacher approach' (2001: 97). She cites technological advancements as the main reason behind this paradigm shift. The SUNY system has included information literacy as one of their core competencies, and the librarians at Cobleskill reasoned that the faculty – 150 strong – were more likely to be able to reach all 2,500 students on campus than their small staff. After trying and discarding two common approaches – an information literacy course taught by librarians, and including IL in a course required for all freshmen – the Cobleskill library staff opted to 'embed information literacy across the curriculum' (98). Students, they reasoned, are more likely to 'take the research skills instruction seriously when taught by their professor' (99). Caveats abound. Will faculty simply teach students how they themselves conduct research? Will only databases related to their discipline be taught? How comfortable are faculty with the technologies involved? Will all faculty be able to provide access to the databases in the classroom while they teach? All the same, Niles believes that 'librarians must give up the idea that only we can teach research skills adequately. We can create a new role for ourselves by supporting faculty in their development and implementation of information literacy instruction' (99).

Ken Kempcke goes even further. He believes that librarians must become leaders on campus. His article, 'The Art of War for Librarians: Academic Culture, Curriculum Reform, and Wisdom from Sun Tzu' is a rallying cry for librarians. Despite being regarded by faculty 'not as colleagues but as info-servers who try to sell IL like life insurance' (2002: 532), librarians can and should play active roles in advising, campus governance, curriculum reform, and search committees. 'It does us no good to tell other faculty how important we are (or should be). We must show them through our leadership in learning communities' (531). Citing the ancient (fourth-century BC) Chinese strategist, he believes 'the highest form of war strategy is to win without fighting' (538). Mere collaboration, he claims, 'is no longer sufficient in today's changing battleground. Perhaps we need to be conquerors' (538).

Working together

While intriguing, the approaches described by Smith, Niles, and Kempcke strike me as idealistic. Faculty, I believe, would rather concentrate on teaching their disciplines; they would rather leave the time-consuming job of educating students in information literacy to librarians, the information professionals. **Dan Mader:** 'I think involving librarians is incredibly important. If they [students] don't know what the potential is, they probably will never come close to it. Librarians know more than anyone else what's there, so it's a big help for students.' And how are faculty to react now if librarians, having stressed the importance of IL, suddenly want to abdicate responsibility for spreading it to faculty? Smith cites a study (Nowakowski, 1993) that indicates that faculty overwhelmingly support information literacy, but supporting an idea and taking responsibility for teaching it are two very different things. As for librarians, many would not, I feel, be comfortable ceding this task to faculty. Would they really take it seriously? As a group – even if primed by librarians – would they present its main tenets consistently? Smith is correct in identifying time constraints of librarians, but would a campus-wide effort such as he proposes really save them time? In conclusion, I can't imagine that faculty would be very happy being told what to teach and how to teach it by a group many do not consider their peers.

I prefer to break up responsibility for teaching IL in the following manner. The primary responsibility for teaching students to *locate information* lies with librarians. Keeping up with all the additions to and changes in information sources is a full-time job. Faculty have little time for this; librarians continually update these skills in order to serve students and faculty. They are responsible for keeping current on databases just as auto mechanics are for the continuing changes in car engines. Yes, there is the occasional faculty do-it-yourselfer who learns the ins and outs of databases, just as there is the odd car owner who changes his own sparkplugs. The overwhelming majority of us, however, turn to experts when we need assistance.

Faculty and librarians need to collaborate closely in the *evaluation of information*. **Tim Lynch** pinpoints one reason for which such collaboration is necessary.

> Unfortunately, they'll [students] take the line of least resistance. They'll do their research by getting on Google. You try to tell the students that if they learn the good tools it will really save them time. The tools are constantly changing, which makes it even more important. I always bring in a librarian to talk to my class when I teach my senior research course. Lots of historical sources have not been digitized, so it's important for them to learn that just bringing up things on a screen is not enough. They've always had the internet; they've always had this immediacy, so it's hard for them to learn that lots of research is grunt work.

To combat such student tendencies, faculty should feel free to call on librarians for help. Again, they have enough trouble squeezing what they want their students to learn about their discipline into a semester. This situation is tailor-made for the use of the kind of website Ragains describes.

Evaluating information

At the College of Mount St. Joseph, librarians Susan Falgner and Cynthia Gregory have designed a series of web pages that help students learn how to better evaluate information. They have designed a list of competencies that serve as a kind of informal pre-test for students. Before turning strictly to the evaluation of information, they first ask students to answer more basic questions. Do they know, for example, how to search FOCUS (our online public access catalog)? How to search periodical databases? How to limit searches on any database? How to interpret a citation? How to request items via interlibrary loan? Questions like these separate novices from more experienced library users. In many cases, such basic competencies need to be covered before progressing to questions that determine their ability to evaluate information. Do they know the difference between a magazine and a journal? Do they know what a peer-reviewed journal is? Can they limit searches to include only peer-reviewed journals? Can they distinguish between an online journal article and a website? Do they know the difference between a primary and a secondary source?

It is the rare undergraduate who can truthfully answer all of these questions affirmatively. Most will need to click on links designed to address these issues. As the web has grown and begun to mature, there are ever greater numbers of sites that are truly scholarly. More and more professors are recognizing the presence of quality, academic-oriented websites and are thus allowing their students to cite them as legitimate sources. Many students, however, are still unable to distinguish between amateurish and accomplished sites. To help students make this distinction, Susan and Cynthia developed a site that is quickly becoming a favorite of faculty. **Jim Bodle:**

> They really need a lot of help. Students approach a problem sometimes by saying: 'I'm trying to write about this issue, and I've found this web site, and I think there's something not quite right about this, but he said this, and it's in print, so it's got to be true.' Within my WebCT courses, I've started setting links to some of these sources on the library's web site.

The site Jim describes is named 'Evaluating Web Sites.' It walks the student through the process of determining the quality of a website. Who is the author of the website? Does the site include an 'Information About this Site' link? What are his credentials? Is he an expert in the field, or simply an enthusiast? Look at the top or bottom of the web page for institution name, author, contact person, creation date, update information, or affiliations. Does the site present facts or opinions? Next, the content of the site is evaluated. Is the information accurate? Is it properly cited? How does the information compare to other sources you've found on the same topic? When was the page created? How often has it been revised? Are the links it includes still valid? The intended audience is then examined. What is the site's purpose? What is the perspective of the site? Are biases apparent? Has it been evaluated in any way by someone other than the author? Students are advised to consult various review services (e.g. available online at *Librarian's Index to the Internet: lii.org*). Many professional journals now regularly review and evaluate Internet resources. Finally, the ease of use and stability of the site are considered. Is an index or table of contents included? Confirm that the site still exists before you cite it!

Another popular initiative at the College of Mount St. Joseph is the creation of 'assignment help' pages. These are websites designed to address assignments that faculty give regularly. In the Mount's Religion 102 course, for example, students are required to write an exegesis of a passage from one of the New Testament gospels. Working with the instructors who teach the course, librarian Susan Falgner designed the site to enable students to actively learn the research process instead of passively listening to a librarian explain the process individually for the umpteenth time. The site walks students through how to find: (1) two articles from different journals on the same passage; (2) one commentary in book form; (3) one Bible commentary from the Reference collection; and (4) a list of good online sources. One disadvantage of this approach is that the web page design process can be very time-consuming. Often the use of an adaptable template can simplify the process.

Sooner, not later?

While opinions vary on the best way to present IL, most agree that exposing students to it in their first year is preferable. This approach ensures that they will at least darken the doors of the library before they are required to conduct any serious research. Some may also lose their fear of using the library or of approaching librarians for help. Recognizing early in the game that their professors collaborate with librarians may also help the way students view them. While it may be unrealistic, one hopes that if students are exposed to the process early enough, they may form good library habits which will make subsequent personal and class instruction easier for librarians. Even on campuses where a freshman year program per se does not exist, librarians should look for opportunities to include an IL component in courses required for all freshmen. Introductory writing courses, for example, are ideal since researching background information is often part of writing argumentative papers. Since most campus libraries collect course syllabi, a librarian should be designated to skim these to determine other opportunities for instruction.

One problem with the first-year approach, of course, is that not all faculty members are willing to cede seat time to the process. 'Buy-in' from faculty tends to be inconsistent. Another factor is whether or not an assignment is linked to the instruction. If students are merely passive spectators while a librarian talks to them, it's unlikely that they will take anything of use away from the session. If faculty include an assignment based on the instruction, on the other hand, students are far more likely to pay attention. Even when accompanying assignments are included, however, they are rarely uniform. This inconsistency leaves librarians short of their real goal. Trying to include everything you want the student to know about the library into one class period is another difficulty. 'Schools providing only one-shot sessions with students stated that they could not integrate such things as critical thinking skills, more in-depth searching techniques, or more active learning exercises' (Malone and Videon, 2003: 11).

Assessment

Assessment of IL skills is very important. Like faculty, librarians must be held accountable for what they are assigned to teach. The literature of assessment is vast and lies outside the scope of this book. In a nutshell, librarians conducting IL must decide exactly what they want to learn from the assessment process. What do they want to measure? Student improvement from beginning to end of one semester? Usefulness of such skills after the student leaves college? Or is determining a baseline the desired outcome? Assessment can be a very time-consuming process; to work most efficiently, it's vital to focus only on the perceived need. Ideally, faculty would work with librarians in the design of the assessment process, setting the stage for future communication and improvements.

Jennifer Dorner, a librarian at Lewis and Clark College, has identified 15 IL competencies that can be assessed. These include:

- explores general information sources to increase familiarity with the topic;
- identifies key concepts and terms that describe the information need;
- identifies the value and differences of potential resources in a variety of formats (e.g. multimedia, database, website, data set, audiovisual, and book);
- identifies the purpose and audience of potential resources (e.g. popular vs. scholarly, current vs. historical);
- differentiates between primary and secondary sources, recognizing how their use and importance vary with each discipline;
- investigates the scope, content, and organization of information retrieval systems;
- selects efficient and effective approaches for accessing the information needed from the investigative methods or information retrieval system;
- identifies keywords, synonyms, and related terms for the information needed;
- selects controlled vocabulary specific to the discipline or information retrieval source;
- constructs a search strategy using appropriate commands for the information retrieval system selected (e.g. Boolean operators, truncation, and proximity for search engines; internal organizers such as indexes for books);
- uses various classification schemes and other systems (e.g. call number systems, or indexes) to locate information resources within the library or to identify specific sites for physical exploration;
- identifies gaps in the information retrieved and determines if the search strategy should be revised;

- differentiates between the types of sources cited and understands the elements and correct syntax of a citation for a wide range of resources;

- examines and compares information from various sources in order to evaluate reliability, validity, accuracy, authority, timeliness, and point of view or bias;

- demonstrates an understanding of what constitutes plagiarism and does not represent work attributable to another as his or her own (2003: 105–6).

Librarians who contributed their specific IL strategies to a compilation, *Training College Students in Information Literacy*, remind their peers to 'focus on the student and what they need and don't focus on yourself and what you want to teach' (Primary Research Group, 2003: 12). Another echoes this thought:

> It is really important to pay attention to what your users tell you that they need. We could have a program that we think is fantastic, but if it doesn't meet their needs it isn't really [a good program]. Just because we do something well it doesn't mean that we are meeting the needs of our users. (30)

Such thoughts touch on the age-old question of whether librarians should teach students what we think they need to know, or simply teach to the assignment that their professors have given them. It is sometimes possible to achieve both goals if you approach the matter delicately enough and not ruffle faculty feathers.

Just as some institutions offer numerous courses by which their students can fulfill a basic writing requirement, so has the University at Albany adopted a system by which their students can meet the school's information literacy requirement during their freshman or sophomore years. These courses must have three common characteristics:

- Classroom activities on finding, evaluating, citing, and using information in print and electronic sources from the university libraries, World Wide Web, and other sources. Courses should address questions concerning the ethical use of information, copyrights, and other related issues that promote critical reflection.

- Assignments, course work, or tutorials that make extensive use of the university libraries, World Wide Web, and other information sources.

Assignments should include finding, evaluating, and citing information sources.

- At least one research project that requires students to find, evaluate, cite, and use information presented in diverse formats from multiple sources and to integrate this information within a single textual, visual, or digital document (available online at: *http://library.albany .edu/usered/faculty/newgencomp.doc*).

Once librarians have helped students locate and evaluate information, the responsibility for helping them *use* it effectively lies mainly with the faculty. Students will learn from them how to incorporate what they have learned into their essays and projects. One technical part of this process where librarians sometimes assist faculty is in helping their students cite their sources properly. In addition to the style manuals housed in print in the Reference collection, many libraries have mounted websites that walk students through how to use the major formats (APA, MLA, Chicago, etc.).

Faculty and the reference desk

While information literacy initiatives dominate the literature of the profession, the reference desk service remains equally important. Indeed, 'reference and instruction are intrinsically linked, complementary, and intertwined services' (Wilson, 1995: 158). The image of someone who knows information sources and is able to help patrons find information on their topics is the archetype of a librarian. Reference courses are required in all library science programs, and while these remain vital, in the academic library 'communicating and cooperating with teaching faculty members are as essential as understanding online resources or any other often-consulted reference tool' (Cardwell, 2001: 254). When faculty know and trust the librarians who assist them, the potential for misunderstandings such as the one described below is greatly reduced.

Students were given an assignment to look for an article on a topic in the *Reader's Guide to Periodical Literature*. When we [reference desk staff] recommended that they utilize an online database due to the speed and ease involved, the students flatly insisted that they were required to use *Reader's Guide*. We asked to see the assignment sheet and upon examination we found using *RGPL* was indeed written in as a required part of their research process. Since our library owns less than one-tenth of the journals listed in the *RGPL* it became exceedingly difficult to meet the needs of these students. (Trinchera, 2000: 21)

When faculty become more acquainted with the skills librarians possess, they will likely encourage their students to use their expertise. While librarians must be careful not to offend faculty by 'telling them what to do,' they can take active steps to help avoid difficult reference desk encounters with students. Librarians at Bowling Green State University, for example, have created a website for faculty, 'Elements of an Effective Assignment,' to help avoid difficult encounters between student and librarian. The website 'alerts instructors to the common pitfalls of research assignments and perhaps helps them develop, plan, and test their assignments before distributing them' (Cardwell, 2001: 258). Christine Larson speaks for all academic librarians when she writes 'I can't help students understand their assignment, do it efficiently, find appropriate materials, or interpret those materials if I don't know the assignment and its goals' (Larson, 1998: 259).

Conclusions

Even before the creation of the Internet, undergraduates struggled to identify and effectively use the information they found in their campus libraries. Today their challenge has been intensified. While most undergraduates view the Internet as a familiar friend, few understand how its creation has further complicated their use of libraries. The good news, however, is that academic librarians seem determined to teach them how to more effectively navigate the enormous world of twenty-first-century information. The faculty, too, recognize the importance of teaching what are now commonly referred to as information literacy skills. This shared resolve represents perhaps the most natural opportunity for faculty and librarians to work together on campus. While methods and philosophies vary greatly, a common aim has been identified: to help today's students learn to effectively find, evaluate, and use information in any form, no matter where they find it. The partnership makes sense: librarians are teachers at heart. Technological advancements are making it possible for librarians to create interactive learning tools that can be used outside the classroom, granting faculty members complete possession of their students' 'seat time.' The momentum of information literacy becoming *the* key component of academic librarianship shows no sign of abating. Such recognition indicates that librarians and faculty must continue to find new ways to cooperate if they are to achieve their shared goal: the information literate student.

4

Other faculty–librarian relationships on campus

'A university is just a group of buildings gathered around a library.' – Shelby Foote

As public expectations for higher education continue to evolve, new roles are emerging for academic librarians. Gone are the days when the librarian's work was constrained within the walls of the library building. Indeed, if today's academic librarians wish to thrive, they must take on duties for which they may not necessarily have been trained. Library directors especially

> must develop their influence both within and outside their domain if they are to ensure that the capabilities of the library are exploited to best advantage and that the capabilities of this, the most traditional of campus services, are fully appreciated. (Williams, 1998: 40)

Though many variations exist throughout the world of higher education, librarians, like faculty, have traditionally reported to the Academic Dean. Since the mid-1990s, however, an increasing number of colleges and universities in the United States have placed the library under the Chief Information Officer (CIO) in their administrative structure. This change resulted mainly from the increasing computerization of libraries and is regarded by some as dangerous. In some sense, such reorganization separates librarians from their traditional partners, the teaching faculty. As we have seen, the faculty are the chief power brokers on campus, and by separating themselves thus from them, librarians risk becoming isolated and less powerful. Especially in these times of rapid change, it is essential that librarians establish and retain an increasingly meaningful role on campus. It is probably too early to speculate further about the impact such a divorce from their faculty colleagues may have on librarians, but it is an issue worth watching in the future. Librarians who do not have faculty status, of course, have long had to deal with these issues.

Under either model, the library director reports to an administrative officer who is part of the President's executive council or advisory group. The director must not only be able to effectively run his own operation, increasingly he and his staff must be willing to become active academic citizens. This means attending faculty or administrative staff meetings, serving on committees, volunteering for taskforces, and generally making themselves available for whatever assignments are open. While the unique status of librarians on campus can sometimes work against them, in campus politics the fact that they are neither teaching faculty nor strictly administrative staff means that these camps often view them as neutrals who can be trusted to make impartial decisions. In the same way, the library building can serve as neutral territory to host informal faculty forums, teaching workshops, and the like.

Serving on campus committees

Following their first year of service, academic librarians who have faculty status are usually eligible to serve on campus committees. Such service 'gives the library visibility, allows for networking within the larger community, lets librarians meet face-to-face with faculty in a setting other than the library, [and] offers an opportunity to slip in advertising for the library's services, etc.' (Alkins, 1996: 652). While early in their careers they must usually be content to serve on lower-level committees, academic librarians should be ambitious enough later on to find spots on more important groups such as the Curriculum Committee. Respect from faculty members comes most easily when they see librarians as true peers who are able to share with them the responsibility of governing the institution.

Mary Kay Fleming elaborates.

> I think one thing that I would hope they'd [new librarians] do is to do what you all do – to be full partners of the faculty. From committee work, to speaking up at meetings. You've done a good job of fully integrating it with teaching, but it might take a person who's aggressively pursuing that to do it. In other words, I could

imagine a librarian who kind of hung back and thought 'when they need me, they'll visit.' I don't think you all do that and I don't think you should. Some new faculty might not come into the situation knowing that you're full partners, but here they will form that impression very quickly. So I would hope that librarians in training develop the mindset that they are full partners, that they deserve to be, and that they should look for opportunities to make that point to faculty.

Many campuses include a Library Committee as part of their institution's governance structure. It is usually composed of at least one student and several junior faculty members and serves as an advisory board of sorts for the director. Topics often brought before the committee include proposed policy changes, departmental allocations and other budgetary matters, journal cancellation projects, adoption of new electronic resources, and the like. While some library directors see it as an important communication medium, others have little use for the library committee and may eventually seek its dissolution. Compared to others on campus, it is generally not regarded as an important committee and usually does not attract influential faculty members. When cordial relations exist between the library and faculty, there is little need for such a group and members' time can best be spent elsewhere. A new library director with little experience in academia, or one who values participative decision-making, however, may find a library committee useful.

Librarians' role in distance education

Distance education is playing an ever greater role in American higher education. According to Michael Moore, then director of the American Center for the Study of Distance Education at Penn State University:

> Distance education is planned learning that normally occurs in a different place from teaching and as a result requires special techniques of course design, special instructional techniques, special methods of communication by electronic and other technology, as well as special organizational and administrative arrangements. (Moore and Kearsley, 1996: 2)

The number of students enrolled in distance education courses grew from 1.3 million in 1997–98 to an estimated 2.9 million in 2000–01 and is even higher today due to the success of institutions such as the University of Phoenix, which offers only 'online degrees.'

Academic librarians can be important partners to faculty who teach distance education courses. Cooperation between the two groups is especially important during the planning phase of such courses. Identification of appropriate online library resources is a vital component to the legitimacy and ultimate success of distance courses. Creating formal resource-sharing agreements with other local libraries that may serve as 'home libraries' for distance students is another element central to the process. As far as possible, librarians need to ensure that distance students have access to the same resources as their traditional peers. Tom Riedel, Distance Services Librarian at Regis University in Denver Colorado, found that before he began working actively with faculty, distance education students were 'presented with a list of potentially frustrating dead ends ranging from inappropriate to plain wrong' (2003: 480). To address the problem, Riedel created a list of 'Recommended Online Resources by Subject.' He then actively 'marketed their focused use in online courses' (481). Greater faculty use of electronic reserves was another strategy Riedel recommended.

Working as part of online course design teams with instructional designers and faculty members, Riedel soon realized that 'faculty were not always aware of the library resources in their own fields and that their expectations of the types of materials that could be culled from library resources were not always realistic' (483). These discussions thus gave him opportunities to better educate faculty as to what the library could and could not do to help their students. Riedel's general hopes were that by being part of the design teams he could ensure that distance students gain easy access to relevant sources, and that 'the library should maintain control of library content by creating separate Web pages linked to each online course' (483).

The library as faculty refuge

While many of the topics in this book have dealt with contemporary developments in library and information science, it is important to remember that no matter how many electronic resources might be added, many faculty still value the library building as a place of refuge. **Elizabeth Barkley** considers the library a central part of the campus, not only for its resources but as a respite spot. If I'm in my office, I'm there for students, so I'm not going to close my door. So often I'll come to the library as a quiet space, a sanctuary sometimes.

This sentiment is echoed by Walt Crawford who believes that 'in addition to collections, libraries provide a place for people to meet, study, read, research, play, and find answers to their questions' (Crawford, 2003: 88). Wayne Wiegand, professor of library and information studies at Florida State University, encourages increased study of the library as place in future library science curricula. He believes that 'by concentrating so much in our research and teaching on information (and especially on the type of information made accessible by computer technology), and by largely overlooking "reading" and "place" in our professional discourse, we deprive ourselves and our students of opportunities to develop a much deeper understanding of the library in the life of the user' (Wiegand, 2005: 61).

After interviewing ten University of Oklahoma faculty, Debra Engel found that they value the library as an 'oasis of solitude' where 'ser endipitous browsing' can take place. There they can write or study in peace, something at a premium in these days of e-mail and cell phones. As a matter of fact, many faculty who have a dedicated library carrel instruct departmental staff not to disclose its location. Engel also includes data drawn from a 2002 Association of Research Libraries (ARL) survey of 112 libraries. Seventy-five per cent of libraries responding noted that they do provide individual study spaces for faculty. Humanities and social science faculty are more likely to use such spaces than colleagues from other disciplines. The popularity of study carrels is underlined by the fact that 22 institutions reported waiting lists for them. Comparing these data to a similar survey conducted in 1968, Engel reports that it is 'striking that so many faculty members still demand space in the library and value this territory so passionately' (2004: 18). Given the fact that the Oklahoma faculty agreed that 'going to the library is a ritual that puts them in the right frame of mind to do serious work' (12), Engel wonders if future generations of scholars who have grown up studying on their PC outside the library will continue to venerate the space. For the time being, however, it seems safe to assume that faculty will appreciate the physical space known as the library for years to come.

Faculty outreach librarians

In the early 1990s, when the Internet was still new, George Washington University (GWU) began a series of workshops designed to instruct faculty in its use. To consolidate their success and to address continuing issues which flowed from these discussions, GWU created the position of Faculty Outreach Librarian (FOL). The primary role of the position was to educate faculty 'on the growing role of information technology in research and teaching and to enhance their support for new electronic resources' (Stebelman et al., 1999: 121). Instead of assigning such roles piecemeal to its entire staff, GWU chose to assign one librarian to organize such efforts. The person chosen to initially fill the position (half-time as FOL and half-time as reference librarian and subject specialist) was experienced and held a doctoral degree, a fact 'which helped the faculty to view him as a peer' (123). One of the FOL's first tasks was to establish an electronic listserv to provide a convenient communication medium for faculty to discuss library issues. One-on-one consultations and informal 'brown bag' lunches were also offered to get the word out. Campus administrators, too, were included as a target audience, due to their role in financing library purchases. 'Because most people respond to new technology when they believe it will simplify their work, personal letters were sent to key administrators (e.g. the president, vice presidents, and deans), indicating the librarians' willingness to teach them Internet skills' (125). Other efforts initiated by the FOL included an annual information technology symposium and focus groups made up of both technophobes and technophiles. GWU identified the following list of traits essential to the success of the FOL:

> ... leadership skills; entrepreneurship; instructional skills to provide workshops and IT demonstrations; comfort communicating with, and approaching, faculty; a willingness to learn and implement different methods of marketing the library's services to faculty and administrators; excellent writing skills, for any newsletters and fliers that are developed; excellent analytical skills to assess what is and is not working and to prepare reports for library administrators; a willingness to be proactive, to seek out users in their offices, parties, and departmental meetings; the ability to work independently, given that many projects will either originate with, or be assigned to, the FOL. (128)

San Jose State University has created a similar position, Outreach Librarian, who is 'responsible for continuously monitoring emerging opportunities for collaboration, taking the lead in laying the ground-work for the new initiatives, and providing support for the ongoing outreach efforts of the librarians' (Breivik and McDermand, 2004: 215).

Learning communities

A significant recent development in higher education is the growth of learning communities.

> A learning community is any one of a variety of curricular structures that link together several existing courses – or actually restructure the curricular material entirely – so that students have opportunities for deeper understanding and integration of the material they are learning, and more interaction with one another and their teachers as fellow participants in the learning enterprise. (Gabelnick et al., 1990: 19)

Librarians can be valuable members of such groups. 'Academic librarians are constantly working with students in the learning mode, and they also work with faculty as faculty recognize that they need to learn new literature for interdisciplinary work or new technologies to be effective in communicating with students' (Reichel, 2001: 819). Learning communities reflect recent trends in higher education, such as the use of WebCT or Blackboard, course management systems that enable faculty to easily put relevant resources online. 'While many faculty were initially concerned that use of technology would make education more impersonal, in fact many have discovered that online components increase the amount and level of social interaction in classes' (Lippincott, 2002: 190). Jack Hettinger confirms this: 'Technology can never be separated from the human personalities. It's the relationship that the teacher has with the students that is fundamental.'

Marketing the library to faculty

The notion of actively marketing an academic library's services would have drawn scant attention twenty years ago. How times change!

It is no longer sufficient for 21st-century academic librarians to simply advertise their services within the physical confines of their buildings. Librarians must take a proactive approach, viewing the strategic marketing of their services and resources as critical to their continued survival. Librarians cannot simply talk about their importance to the 'learning community,' they must become a part of it, actively learning the skills needed to market their libraries. (Cawthorne, 2003: 667)

Inspired by the Internet's challenge to their information supremacy, academic librarians have begun to realize that they must promote their products just like any other business. As the professorate – not to mention administrators and students – grows ever more comfortable with the Internet, these efforts must continue if we want to stop reading about the decline and ultimate obsolescence of academic libraries. In 2003, the American Library Association (ALA) published a marketing 'toolkit' to help librarians promote their libraries. As the toolkit points out, librarians are their own best advocates. It is up to us to educate those who do not use our resources to the extent that we believe they should. While this group is mostly made up of students and administrators, librarians should not neglect to extend similar efforts toward faculty. It is, after all, the faculty who largely drive student use of the library; it is faculty who support librarians in their efforts to justify to administrators our ever increasing budgets.

In their toolkit, ALA underlines three important messages librarians must promote. The first is that 'college and research libraries are an essential part of the learning community' (6). After the classroom, the library is the next most important place where campus learning takes place. The second is that libraries 'connect you with a world of knowledge' (7). Thanks to technological advances and the cooperative ethos of librarians, this message is more literally true than ever before. Perhaps students don't appreciate this to the extent they should; perhaps, to make them more appreciative, faculty should describe the 'primitive' conditions under which they researched their dissertations. The third message is that academic libraries 'are investing in the future, while preserving the past' (7). Digitization has made preservation efforts much more accessible than in earlier eras. Old treasures must no longer be protected or hidden from potential users, present and future.

Librarians must continually stress to their patrons the advantages of using the library over the Internet. Mark Herring's article, '10 Reasons

Why the Internet is No Substitute for a Library' provides as good a place as any to start. While this article applies mainly to undergraduate use of the Web, faculty may learn a thing or two from it as well which – if they want to receive better papers – they will pass on to their charges.

1. Contrary to undergraduate belief, 'not everything is on the Internet' (2001: 76). Students are often unaware of the existence of propri-etary databases or their cost. They have grown up using a largely 'free' Internet and sometimes don't realize that not everything they find on the Web is free. As their research needs progress, they need to learn how well the library is using their tuition dollars; they need to learn the value of these expensive products and how they differ in purpose and quality from mere websites. Also important to advertise is the fact that even when libraries have purchased subscriptions to electronic journals individually or via aggregated databases, these constitute only a fraction of the number of journals still available only in print.

2. Let students joke all they want about the Dewey Decimal or Library of Congress classification systems, when they encounter the primi-tive means by which Yahoo and other search services have at-tempted to catalog the Web, they may gain a new appreciation for the efforts of Melvin Dewey.

3. One lesson students should learn from librarians' information liter-acy efforts is that, on the Web, 'quality control doesn't exist' (77). There is no editor for the Internet. If you have access to server space, you, too, can be 'published.'

4. While the situation has improved since Herring's article was first published, full-text journals still do not always exactly duplicate all the features of their print equivalents. Graphics, tables, and the like may not appear in the full-text version seen on screens.

5. Yes, the full-text of many literary classics published before 1925 are available on the Web, but they constitute the merest fraction of the millions of books published in the twentieth century alone.

6. Even when full-text is found on the Web, it is nowhere near as com-fortable to read as an old-fashioned book. Again, this situation has begun to improve, but until monitor design improves, online readers will continue to suffer eye strain.

7. A completely virtual library is still an impossibility. That is, elec-tronic resources are important to every library, but they cannot stand alone.

8. A variation on number seven's theme, digitizing everything college students need in order to create a 'virtual state library' which would serve everyone remains prohibitively expensive.
9. 'Not much on the Internet is more than 15 years old' (78). This might sound like an advantage to some young minds, but we must remind students that those who do not study the past are doomed to repeat it.
10. Finally, people still enjoy the portability and convenience – not to mention the aesthetics – of the book.

Librarians should share Herring's article with their patrons. It should prove a catalyst for active discussion. The ALA marketing toolkit suggests other ways to keep the library in the public eye.

- Hold marketing events in the facility during National Library Week. Try to accommodate as many faculty as possible by offering workshops in varying time frames and feed them at such events whenever possible. Season your messages or presentations with humor. Be careful not to bombard your audience with statistics. Define library jargon for them so that the impact of your message isn't minimized.

- Create separate budget lines for marketing efforts. Look into purchasing pens, water bottles, mouse pads and the like that include your library's URL and give them away at campus events.

- Share with faculty the kinds of courses you took in graduate school to better acquaint them with librarianship. Many may still wonder why librarians even need a graduate degree to perform their jobs.

- Stress that any investment in the library is an investment for the whole college.

- Develop a quarterly communication medium to keep faculty up to date on the latest changes in the library.

- Consult with marketing professionals on campus who may be able to provide other good suggestions. Whatever method you choose to get the message out, don't be afraid to blow your own horn a bit. Librarians have kept their skills under wraps for far too long.

Other ways to reach your faculty

The ideas listed below stem from a variety of sources. Some are my own, but most originated with other academic librarians. An excellent place to start the discussion is Terri Holtze's list of '100 Ways to Reach Your Faculty' which she compiled based on her own ideas and a literature search on the topic. Holtze, Reference and Instruction Librarian at the University of Louisville, first presented a list of '50 Ways' at the 2001 Association of College and Research Libraries (ACRL) conference in Denver. One year later she fleshed out the list to '100 Ways' as part of the American Library Association pre-conference on adult literacy and outreach in libraries. I am listing below only a few of the most interesting examples from her list. When not Holtze's own, the original source is listed in parentheses.

- Give new faculty a small amount of money to buy library materials they or their students will need.
- Host a 'published this year' party including librarians who have published.
- Write a profile of a faculty member's contribution to library services for the library's newsletter.
- Hold office hours in the department's offices (Susan Wolf Neilson, North Carolina State University).
- Take a class in their department.
- Ask to observe class sessions to gain a better understanding of the topics covered.
- Catalog their personal or office collections.
- Put together a seminar for faculty on detecting plagiarism (Barbara Hightower, West Texas A&M University).
- Work together on a bibliography.
- Create an annual award for the faculty member who has done the most to collaborate with or promote the library.

The University of Illinois at Urbana-Champaign (UIUC) has devised another way to improve the library's relationship with faculty. Since 'achievement of tenure and promotion in rank may constitute the single most significant event in the professional life of a faculty member' (German and Schmidt, 2001: 1066), UIUC allows newly tenured faculty to select a book for inclusion in its permanent collection. The library then includes a bookplate for this work that marks the accomplishment. 'Faculty are encouraged to select titles that represent something meaningful to them, either professionally or personally' (1067). Alice Harrison Bahr of Salisbury University (Maryland, USA) suggests purchasing two copies of every book authored by faculty members. One copy is placed in the circulating collection, the second in a non-circulating 'Faculty Collection.' Such a collection can be an impressive stop on library tours and during accreditation visits. Librarians should continually be thinking of small gestures like this that can cultivate their alliance with instructors.

Even simple gestures like hosting a luncheon for new faculty members at the beginning of an academic year can go far to foster good relationships with teaching colleagues. While faculty eat, librarians can introduce themselves and sneak in some plugs for library services. The beginning of a faculty member's tenure is a very important time for librarians to establish a relationship. At Western Michigan University, this idea has been taken a step farther. There a librarian takes new faculty members out to lunch individually. 'Even if they are not newly hatched from graduate school, asking about their dissertation is still a good way to make them feel at ease' (Isaacson, 2001: 532).

A reader's advisory service is often popular with both faculty and staff. They love to 'talk books' with librarians and this service can be a good bridge-builder. At my institution I have created a monthly feature for our website, 'Books with POJ,' that serves this purpose. An example is offered below.

> This month's book is *Ahab's Wife, or The Star-Gazer* (1999, 666 pages) by Sena Jeter Naslund. 'Captain Ahab was neither my first husband nor my last.' Such is the arresting first sentence of Naslund's historical novel. Narrated in the first person, *Ahab's Wife* tells the remarkable tale of Una Spenser, a strong, adventurous woman who is more than a match for the captain of the Pequod. By the time she weds Ahab, Kentucky-born Una has already run away from home, stowed away on a whaler, survived a shipwreck which forces her into cannibalism, and dealt with the death of both her mother and her infant daughter. If all this sounds a bit sensational, be assured that the author's sturdy prose keeps the story from lapsing into melodrama. This ambitious novel succeeds as both a stirring tale and a look into numerous issues facing women in 19th century America.

Catherine Cardwell (2001: 261–2) lists the following strategies for becoming better acquainted with faculty.

- Create a faculty guide detailing the types of instructional services you offer as well as contact information. The guide should be available both in print and online.

- Advertise new and changing resources and services. Check on your campus to see if a faculty listserv or newsletter is available. Update faculty in a timely way.

- Surf faculty web pages in your assigned subject area to discover their research interests. Try to make contact with those faculty teaching research courses or those faculty whose research interests relate to your own.

Texas Woman's University has created a Faculty Information Research Service Team (FIRST) to meet their faculty's information needs. Faculty members were interviewed to identify how the library could best assist them.

> The findings affirmed the value of the FIRST program's basic tenet, namely that personalized service that maximizes mass-customization options (such as TOC [table of contents] messages and document delivery systems) is a sound basis on which to build a responsive program. The findings also suggested an additional range of services that might be offered to faculty including: assistance in developing a personal information management system; on-demand, highly focused information coaching or instruction via multiple delivery methods; and a series of progressively advanced instructional efforts that lead to a greater level of self-sufficiency in managing digital information, such as Web sites and full-text documents. (Westbrook and Tucker, 2002: 148)

Conclusions

When librarians play active roles on campus they help keep the library vibrant and vital. In the minds of far too many members of the campus community, Larry Hardesty notes, an academic library is not the heart of an institution, it is its spleen. That is, 'many undergraduates barely know it exists, few know its purpose, and most could live without it' (Hardesty, 1991: 126). Establishing active relationships with the faculty members who guide student learning is the best way to change this perception and return the library to a more central part of an institution's anatomy.

In order to effect this change, academic librarians must play roles that have not been traditional in the profession. They must become more extroverted, more willing to serve the campus as true academic citizens, and not just as librarians. While committee membership is the most obvious way to achieve this goal, numerous others exist. Librarians need be limited only by their imaginations. They must study marketing techniques and determine which might be effective on their campus. The advent of distance education programs presents librarians with another opportunity to assist their institution. In the last few decades, the world of higher education has shown that, contrary to its traditional image, it is willing to embrace change. Indeed, it must continue to adapt and take chances if it is to survive. As members of the academic community, librarians must be willing to as well, or risk being left behind.

5

Interviews with College of Mount St. Joseph faculty

During the summer of 2004 I interviewed 15 faculty members from my institution. These instructors represent ten different disciplines and range in rank from Assistant Professor to Professor. It is my hope that potential academic librarians who read these transcripts will gain a better idea of who faculty are, what concerns they have, and how they interact with librarians. Portions of the interviews have been included as quotes in earlier chapters of this work.

Elizabeth Barkley, Professor, Department of Humanities

Q: What are the major sources of stress in your job?

A: Trying to find a balance between committee work and citizenship, teaching, and scholarly and creative activity. Trying to find an appropriate balance is hard, especially at a teaching college. We bill ourselves here primarily as teachers, but we also need to be part of the community.

Q: Can you estimate what percentage of your time is spent in each one of these activities?

A: I would say teaching 60 per cent, service 30 per cent, and scholarship 10 per cent. I don't like that balance, but it's the one we have here.

Q: What would you prefer?

A: A 60:20:60 split would be better. As a tenured department member in a department that has a lot of junior faculty, I make it a point to jump in and do a lot of the department work. They can get overwhelmed. So in a sense my citizenship work is self-imposed. These jobs are not forced on me.

Q: What are some popular misconceptions that the general public has about college faculty?

A: That we have a lot of free time, and that once you've taught a class all you do is go in and do the same thing again so you don't have any preparation. Whereas every time I teach a class, even if I use the same text, I tend to recreate the class, to build upon experiences from the last time, or to make it fresher.

Q: Can you estimate how many hours you work in a typical week?

A: I'd say I'm on campus most days from 8:30 until 5:00, and then I work evenings and much of my weekend. I do have a social life and a family, too, though. I think it's easier at a large research university to come in, teach classes, have a few office hours, and then spend the rest of the day working at home, or working in the library. On this campus, though, it seems that something bleeds into the next thing, and all of a sudden it's five o'clock. I might have planned to go home at 2:00 or 3:00 to get some reading done.

Q: How different is the job from your original expectations?

A: I thought I'd have more time during the academic year and the summer to really do class reading and explore background material. It's practically a 12-month job now and we're not on a 12-month contract. That's a big issue that we as a faculty have to confront very soon. Some of this, again, is due to personal choices. I taught a summer class that ended in June, then I taught a one-week summer institute which I really wanted to teach because it was team-taught. I teach a class called 'Exploring the Sacred' with a theology professor. I don't get a chance to do many courses like this because I have so many core, required courses I have to teach. We have a cooperative education program and in the summer, I have two or three students in that I have to supervise. We have a new freshman registration system. Instead of having students come in big groups on certain days, we are pretty much available to come in during the summer when they make their decision to register.

Q: Can you take me through your formal education, beginning with your entry into graduate school?

A: I did a Master's program in American Studies over four summers while I was teaching in high school. I got that in 1976. I continued to teach high school and then ended up working for a newspaper for three years later on. I began as an adjunct here while my children were still young, so that worked out nicely. I did adjunct teaching and free-lance writing. About twelve years into being an adjunct, the department chair told me he had a chance to slip me in as a full-time faculty member. At that point I was told that if I wanted to continue and move into a full-time position then I would need to get my doctorate. I started it in '92 and had it by '97.

Q: How important is collaborating with campus librarians to help students learn research skills?

A: Students generally come to the College not having read a lot and not having had to use the resources of a library. They've learned to navigate the Web pretty successfully, but most of them are not familiar with the library. What's on your website is very helpful. Students want to use their computers, so I try to show them that there are already a lot of really good resources on there. We've been talking about students, but I could not have done my doctoral dissertation without this library. Anyway, I've also used librarians for instruction, coming into my classes to do modules. The other thing I'd say is that when I've needed things quickly – videos and CDs especially – the library has been instrumental in getting them on time. It's very important to integrate multimedia into instruction.

Q: How important is the library in the student's life? That is, how important should it be compared to how important it actually is?

A: I think it should be important. When we get to our senior projects in our majors, we begin to realize how little they've used the library up to that point. That appalls us considering we have built in – we thought – assignments or projects that should have had them use the library. Most of them know about OhioLINK, but most don't realize they can download full-text articles. I feel really bad that somehow they get to be a senior and then their senior project becomes not a demonstration of how well they can do this, but almost a place to learn this! We really have to work on that, building it in all along. I also try to tell students that librarians get excited about helping them. When they experience this, it's an awakening to them. I wish that students had the experience I had of just going up to the stacks and paging through books. It's a very rich experience. A number of them don't have time to do that, or they don't care.

Q: With the advent of OhioLINK making it so easy to get books sent here from around the state, have you recommended fewer titles for the local collection here?

A: I think I still recommend a lot of books for our library here. There's nothing like having it on the shelf. I know that there are budget constraints. I think the more frustrating thing is that we don't have the money to purchase larger journal collections.

Q: What are some adjectives that you believe apply to a successful faculty member?

A: Energetic, inquiring, open-minded, collaborative, well-rounded, creative, critical.

Q: Have you seen a change in your students since you first started teaching here?

A: They seem more stressed. They're not as eager to really immerse themselves in the educational experience. They want to get through the steps to get the degree. They're focused on getting a job. Some of it comes from time constraints. I hate to dump on standardized testing, but these are the first students who have been through 12 years of stan- dardized testing, and they are goal-oriented in the sense of 'I've got to pass this test' rather than being able to really get excited about learning. The whole system of education has become so 'fill in the blank' that – and I'm not faulting teachers, I'm faulting legislatures for that – naturally they're goal-oriented.

Q: How do you feel about the new emphasis on accountability in higher education?

A: It's a slippery slope from what's happening in grade school. They might not be holding us accountable for things that are valid. It's started in primary and secondary schools and now it's coming up. See, I think a lot of things that happen in higher education are not measur- able, tied to learning outcomes and performance indicators. That's a really scary trend, to think that we can reduce a college education – which used to be this mind-opening, broadening, liberal arts, life- changing experience – into checking off skills rather than developing habits of mind.

Q: Is this trend coming from the accrediting bodies?

A: I think the accrediting bodies are feeling pressure from consumers and politicians, and it's tied into the cost of education. As you pay more and more you want to get something for your money that's got to be measurable. I don't know what's driving up the cost of education. Maybe it's all the technology. It's scary to me that so many students are not going to be able to afford an education, or that they're going to be so in debt by the time they graduate that they're not going to be able to buy a home or raise children.

Q: What are the possible roles of technology in higher education, both as you've used it and in general?

A: I can't imagine a library that's not computerized. The speed with which you can find resources and get to them beyond the campus has just totally transformed how we can do research and how we can teach. I think students probably need to understand in a broader way what technology can do rather than just learning how to use a particular resource. We are a wired campus. All my writing and speech classes are totally computer-based. I give them links they can go to, they submit assignments electronically. I use WebCT in what I think is a balanced way. It can be used so intensely that it becomes a burden. I use it to post syllabi, get discussion groups going, and even set up special discussion groups among students so that they don't always have to meet. The nice thing is when they use it for things that aren't required, to communicate to one another or to share ideas. In my journalism classes the technology is very helpful. Their assignment might be to go to a newspaper online and then talk to their group about why they chose that particular paper. It's transformed the class completely. One downside of technology is that students expect you to instantly respond to them when they send you something electronically. They become very impatient. They're used to using Instant Messenger, text messaging on phones, and so on.

Q: How important is the library to your academic well-being?

A: I consider the library a central part of the campus, not only for its resources but as a respite spot. If I'm in my office, I'm there for students, so I'm not going to close my door. So often I'll come to the library as a quiet space, a sanctuary sometimes.

Q: How will libraries change in the future?

A: I think they've already begun the change. Rather than be a repository of books that can be checked out, I think they are a resource center for any kind of publication or multimedia. The greatest thing librarians could do would be to make themselves accessible and to let people know that they don't just want to sit behind their desk, that they're in this field because they love to learn, they love to research, and they love to find answers. Our librarians do that well, but I don't think that's true for other libraries, especially public libraries.

Q: Any final thoughts?

A: I think if you're aiming this book at future librarians, they should really consider working in an academic library because it's a very energizing atmosphere to be in. It's a stable, returning population compared to, let's say, that of a public library. In a library like ours you can build peer relationships.

Q: Do you think faculty members look at librarians as peers?

A: I think once people have had interactions with the librarians, they gain great respect for them. We see them as support, but we don't look down on them. It's a different job on campus that can be a great help to us.

Jim Bodle, Associate Professor, Behavioral Sciences Department

Q: What are the major sources of stress in your job?

A: I would say the multiple demands. It seems to me that faculty serve a role that's in part administrative and in part teaching, and this is paired against the demand for scholarship, advising students, running a department or program, and service demands such as being on committees. It's a lot to juggle all at the same time. To do any one of these effectively is pulling time away from something else you'd rather be doing. Today there are also lots of demands that come with technology. It's so hard now to teach a class with integrity when you might be second-guessing a student for things like plagiarism. It's become like a second job, just to try to outstep where the students are going to go in terms of finding a paper. It's a nightmare.

Q: What are some of the other downsides to using technology in the classroom?

A: Technology is at least a double-edged sword. One of the problems that you run into with technology is that I don't know that we all have sufficiently adapted what we do to really take advantage of the technology. Sometimes students just get bored and here's this thing in front of them, and the professor's not really asking them to do anything with it, but there are competing temptations. I find that if you are able to deliberately tell students to do something in class, then the inappropriate use will go down. In my Introduction to Psychology course, for instance, we used to do a lot of these little surveys that were a very short personality inventory, and the student would have to do that manually in class and score it and that would begin the discussion in class about the topic. Carolyn Boland [the College's webmaster] has helped me be able to make those into instantly scoring HTML documents. Now I can say, 'link to the WebCT calendar today. The survey's there. Complete it now and it will give you the score.' Right there they're doing something that's saving paper, giving them the instant score, and it's using technology to do the very thing I wanted them to do. So some of the responsibility lies with the faculty member adapting to the technology. Students can find all sorts of ways of outsmarting us.

Q: In a book titled *The Professors: Who They Are, What They Do*, the author, Herbert Livesey, states 'For some time, the American college professor has been the most pampered professional in our society.' What's your reaction to that statement?

A: We're pampered? I'd like to know when the pampering starts.

Q: Some of the arguments that he uses are that (a) faculty receive higher than average salaries for a shorter working year; (b) good financial aid packages are available for graduate study; (c) they pay no rent for office space, secretarial staff, etc., as other professionals do; (d) their great flexibility of schedule; (e) tenure as such doesn't exist in other professions; (f) they receive good benefit packages from their employer.

A: The whole notion of tenure as he might have seen it is out of date. The days of spending five or six years in a tenure track job, then going for tenure and getting it and never having to worry about another performance evaluation are long gone. We're on a five-year post-tenure review cycle. It's not as large a process as the tenure decision is, but you still need to be performing in all the major areas. It's just that the package is not as large. Every five years you have to show that you're still performing well in the classroom and getting good evaluations; you still have to show that you've been keeping current in your field and making revisions to your courses; you have to document that you've still been publishing or doing other creative or scholarly work on an ongoing basis. And the list goes on. They want to see that it's a growing, maturing, more complete process, it's not the same standard as it is the first time you went up. And you need to be serving the College. You can't just check out. His comment is based really on a stereotype of faculty life and not at all the real demands. I almost feel like it's not a ten-month contract anymore. There are so many demands. Faculty are becoming more a part of the management of the college in some ways in that we're always on call. The changes in our student body means that you have to be on call all the time if a potential student wants to come on campus for a visit, or for advising a current student. We do rope off certain days during the summer where someone from the department will be on campus, but sometimes students come on other days. I understand this from a marketing standpoint, but in terms of really doing the work that you think of as being your academic work, it's a big challenge. More and more we're being expected to fill certain hours.

Q: What about the issue of accountability? There's been a growing movement of trying to hold higher education more accountable. How has that affected your work?

A: It's everywhere. It has changed how you structure a syllabus in that there have to be very clearly outlined learning outcomes. In planning a syllabus you have to plan in opportunities for students to be able to show that they have begun in a certain place, and then throughout the course acquired these skills at varying levels. So what you do in class is going to be different. You can't lecture, but you have to focus much more heavily on doing activities within the class that will allow students to show their changing understanding. That's a completely different focus from what it used to be.

Q: When you were in graduate school, planning on becoming an instructor at the college level, how different were your expectations of the job from what it's really like?

A: The graduate program does not help you to know how to do that kind of accountability. One of my big pet peeves is that people don't understand what a graduate degree is. I think that that influences a lot of attitudes that people have about what a degree really means. Let's face it, there are completely different goals for a bachelor's degree than for any Master's degree or doctoral degree of any kind. The work of a Master's or doctoral degree is to focus you in a specific area so that you think like a member of that discipline, which is not what you're supposed to do in a bachelor's degree program. Some students think that because you have a PhD you should know everything and that's actually just the opposite. You should know a great deal about this itty-bitty piece of the world. I'd love it if people knew that. Most graduate programs do not help you learn effective ways of teaching students and meeting the kind of objectives you need to in higher education. The focus is on research and scholarship, not on teaching. In fact, in some programs they almost discourage you from teaching because you really need to be focusing on becoming a scholar in that area. In my program it was a requirement by your third year to be teaching, but there was very little training for that. I sought out opportunities in my first and second year just as a way of trying to gain the skills, but I had to seek out those opportunities. The focus of the one seminar we had on teaching was much more on how to be a professor at a large university where you'd go in and deliver your lecture to 300 people at a time and give two exams and that's it, and that's not at all what we do here. You know, the other piece about accountability that we need to think about is that within a course there are certain learning objectives, but also a department or program has learning objectives. So once the program sets what those objectives are going to be – which are often from a larger body like the American Psychological Association – then you have to map out your curriculum of courses and show that these certain skills, or knowledge, or content areas are being addressed. That has changed to a certain extent what many people would call academic freedom in that you're not entirely free to set any goal in a course. The course typically has to meet certain objectives for the program and so you can't just do whatever you want. Within the program there are demands from the college itself, from the liberal arts and sciences core and so on.

Q: Can you take me through your formal education after you received your undergraduate degree?

A: I followed what really is a pretty unusual path, but what is kind of the mold of what people say you should do. Granted, I didn't have a lot of fun. I did not do anything fun for five years [laughs]. I had the luxury of doing it this way because at that time I was not married and I didn't have a lot of other obligations. When I graduated with my bachelor's degree I applied to a program that focuses very heavily on recruiting students with just bachelor's degrees. That's not as common anymore, but that's the way I did it. I spent two years working on my graduate level course work, reading for the content area where I wanted to write my Master's thesis, and eventually writing a proposal, because my area in psychology is at the scientific research area of discipline. After completing all of the course work and the thesis, I earned my Master's degree. By the time that I defended the Master's thesis, it was two and a half years. Then, I advanced to doctoral candidacy, at which time I started drawing up my content areas for my qualifying exams. That involved working with faculty on a committee to draw up a list of books and articles that would define three major content areas and then a general psychology breadth of knowledge and general methodology knowledge. Approval of the list came within half of a year, then I spent a year reading and studying from this list and taking a few more courses in experimental methodology. Finally, I took my qualifying exams. This involved two days of sitting in a room for eight hours having questions passed to me under a door. I'd type away on a computer for eight hours. It was like being in prison or something! After another week or two they gave me their feedback and then gave me a three-hour oral exam. They wanted me to be able to speak to any specific issues they thought were any weaknesses they'd seen from my written answers. But they also asked completely off-the-wall questions that were just tangents of that. After that I was qualified to write a proposal for the dissertation. I finished the dissertation from beginning to end in six months. That was divine inspiration! Mine was an experimental dissertation and they tend to be shorter. Altogether it was only 65 pages. A lot of the work was coming up with the design, compiling a comprehensive literature review to make sure that it was something that hadn't been done yet – a lot of it is in the experimental work you do to produce the document. Thankfully, I had a readily available population. Also a lot of the work from the comprehensive exams informed how I wrote the proposal, and the body of the proposal became a significant part of the dissertation. So altogether it took me five years after my BS to get the doctoral degree.

Q: Can you describe either negative or positive experiences you've had with librarians throughout your academic career?

A: Most of the negative things that have happened to me in college and university libraries are things that don't happen anymore. Technology has changed the way that we use the library and the way the library responds to our needs. The worst problems that I ran into were just not being able to find certain sources, journals that weren't held locally and were far enough away that I couldn't drive there.

Q: This would be in the early '90s, and the library didn't do inter-library loan for you?

A: They said they didn't do that for graduate students. You've no idea how good the library is here. The other bad story that I have is that during my undergraduate days the library changed from the Dewey Decimal classification system to Library of Congress, and they just left it all in the two different systems. It was really difficult to find anything, because you were always going back and forth between the two systems. The older books stayed in Dewey Decimal and the new ones were cataloged in the Library of Congress system.

Q: They never had a plan to comprehensively convert everything to Library of Congress?

A: There was no plan at the time for ever doing that.

Q: How important is collaborating with campus librarians in helping students learn research skills in your field?

A: I think that a lot of faculty – and I'm speaking a little more broadly than just our campus – just think that you send students off someplace and that some magical librarian will solve all their problems. One of the biggest stumbling blocks is that it's important to know who the librarian is. You need to be able to tell students in very specific ways how to access the library because students for about the last five years or so have known less and less about any library. It seems to me that some students don't even know that there is a library. They think that nothing exists if it's not on the Internet. I'm surprised at the number of students who have never had the experience of having their parents take them to a public library, and many high schools don't even have libraries now! I've been amazed recently with the need to educate students about what a library is, how it works, and what role it should play in thinking about and addressing a problem. At various times I've either taken a class to the library, or had a librarian come talk to the class, or I've used materials that librarians have prepared for these purposes. Susan Falgner [Head of Public Services] has done a wonderful job of putting together very focused sets of resources and guidelines. Within my WebCT courses I've started setting links to some of these sources on the library's website. Students approach a problem sometimes by saying: 'I'm trying to write about this issue, and I've found this website, and I think there's something not quite right about this, but he said this, and it's in print, so it's got to be true.' They really need a lot of help. Every semester I have to spend time talking about the differences between how something gets on the Internet compared to the peer review process or a scholarly review. Students don't seem to have a sense that any of that is any different. I've even had the problem where students have not been able to differentiate between an abstract and a full article. 'It's short, and it didn't give me enough detail,' they'll say. And I'll say, 'that's because it's an abstract!' And students need to know how to use a thesaurus, because often the difference between finding a mediocre source and a good source is finding the right word to search with. I've begun slating a day when students are all supposed to bring their laptops to class and we'll spend the day looking for sources. I'll walk around the room talking to them about certain strategies, like finding one good article and checking what words were used as descriptors for it and using them for their search.

Q: Any final thoughts?

A: It's important for librarians to understand the campus that they're working on; especially on the smaller campuses they need to be willing to be responsive to the faculty's needs. It can be difficult being on a small campus and trying to do a piece of research and not being able to find an article or a book. That's not something we have an issue with here. If we ask for something it's there, faster than you ask for it half the time. But I know that's not always the case on some campuses. On a small campus your collection will resemble the faculty on your campus. One of the biggest roles a librarian can play today is educating some faculty as to the different ways of accessing some material. A lot of older faculty may not know how useful a full-text online source might be, that that can be a better way of meeting the needs of your faculty than actually subscribing to the journal in print. The library's resources really are your faculty's lifeline – 70 per cent to 80 per cent anyway – to the community beyond that college. Today what this means is less having a good collection and more having a good system of interlibrary loan. Obviously, faculty should be members of their professional organizations, but in a small college they may not be able to go to the meetings very often.

Q: We're lucky to have OhioLINK.

A: I don't know how we'd make it without it. The other issue that we ran into until recently is that some disciplines are a lot slower to go online than others. The APA was one of those, until maybe about two or three years ago.

OhioLINK's method is to make contracts with publishers to gain access to all of their journals. They did that with the APA and the American Chemical Society in the last few years. It's a series of negotiations.

Alan de Courcy, Associate Professor in Religious Studies

Q: What are the major sources of stress in your job?

A: Time. There's never enough time to really be prepared. Now, how much of that is an illusion, I'm really not sure. But with committee work, class prep, and other things like that you just don't have enough time. A second source of stress is a sort of creative stress: continually trying to adapt your course material to the level of your students. A number of new faculty here have come in with fairly high expectations and then struggled with trying to teach certain things, and find it's just not getting across. How do you get it down to their level? Thirdly, I think the whole tenure process is a huge stress for people. I've been on both sides of that. I've been on the tenure committee now for five years. Over and over again it hits me how stressful the whole process is. Sometimes the anticipation of what that will be like makes it worse than it actually is.

Q: Please take me through your education after you finished your undergraduate degree.

A: I went directly from my undergraduate education to the University of Chicago with no break in between. I entered what was at that point a doctor of ministry program, but it was a two-year/four-year program, where after two years you got your Master's of Theology and then if you went two years more and completed your thesis you received your doctorate in ministry. I went straight through and got my Master's in two years, but then I got married and got involved in hospital chaplaincy. I was burned out on education, on being a student. I did some work towards the doctor of ministry piece, but didn't complete that at the University of Chicago. Later I got a full-time job as a campus minister at Miami University in Oxford [Ohio]. During all this time I was doing some educational things, becoming certified professionally for things, but not pursuing the degree. I got my Master's in 1970 and then about 1982 or so I made a decision to complete the doctor of ministry work. At that point I enrolled at the United Theological Seminary in Dayton, OH. That was a very self-directed program. I found it much, much harder to do the work on a part-time basis.

Q: You were working full time when you entered that program?

A: Yes. I thought it would take me a couple of years, but it ended up taking me about five or six years. So that was the educational process. I don't recommend this approach necessarily, but it worked for me.

Q: Why did you decide to get back into the teaching side of things?

A: Part of it was that I've always been interested in the educational side of things. So when I was doing the hospital ministry and pastoral counseling with someone, I began doing more and more of what I would call teaching-type workshops. I was also beginning to do more teaching of chaplains. I did a small amount of adjunct teaching as well. I had been listening as a counselor for a long time and felt I had something to say. I was a listener who wanted to start doing some talking! I found that when I began doing my teaching I really liked it. It seemed to be a very good fit for me. A half-time position opened here, and I took that for a year, then it moved to a full-time position. I've been very, very pleased with this position. I have a great department chair.

Q: And that eliminates another possible source of stress?

A: Exactly. So I've never regretted the shift.

Q: Comment on this statement. Since it's so easy to request inter-library loan books via OhioLINK, I request fewer books for permanent addition to our local collection.

A: I agree, because it makes sense. Having this kind of access through OhioLINK is incredible, especially at a small institution like ours. There are things like videos that I still feel it's important for us to get, but it doesn't make sense to me that we try to build up a big collection of books any more. I find that OhioLINK works wonderfully well.

Q: Speaking in general terms, do you think college teachers are paid enough?

A: No [laughs]. I think in comparison to other professionals similarly – or even less well – qualified I think it shows a value system in society that doesn't make a lot of sense. I think college teachers get a bad rap in the sense that they seem to be working less hard than they actually work. There's this sort of myth that you're paying them to just do their own thing. There is a sort of a PR problem in that I feel college teachers do have to deal more fully with the issue of accountability. I think there's been a lot of resistance to doing that. It's happening more – I've just been reading an article about this – but it's happening because rather than choosing to be accountable they're being forced to be accountable.

Q: In a book titled *The Professors: Who They Are, What They Do*, the author, Herbert Livesey, states 'For some time, the American college professor has been the most pampered professional in our society.' What's your reaction to that statement?

A: I think it's a myth. I'll certainly admit that having tenure is a great thing to have, but it's not something that comes easily. To say they're pampered, though ... there are all kinds of stuff that professors have to do. You have to stay current in your field; you have to meet the needs of your students. My guess is that that idea has a lot to do with the idea of tenure. People see that job security as something professors have that no other profession has. But there's a reason for giving people tenure. It's the nature of the profession and being able to do it adequately. It's a matter of academic freedom. Now I think that one of the key issues in education today – and this gets back to the accountability issue – I think what people outside the academy complain about is that the high paid professors at larger institutions end up doing research and not teaching. I think that's changing because of the accountability issue, but I do think that it's a problem when people who are being paid to teach pass that teaching off to graduate assistants and don't teach. In a school like ours, that doesn't happen. The best teachers teach.

Q: Has it been stressful for you to incorporate educational technology into your teaching?

A: That's a great issue. And the answer is yes, definitely. I love technology. I was one of the first faculty on campus to get my website up and I was very excited about it. I still am, but the downside of technology in the classroom has not yet really begun to be dealt with. I think there's a real question if in the end the downside will outweigh the benefits. I think it can be every bit as much a distraction as it can help. Every teacher I talk to now asks 'what do you do to get your students to not use their laptops in class?' My policy on this – and I put this in my syllabus – is that unless I've told you to take out your computer, the computer needs to be closed – without exceptions. Now I've had students come to me and say 'we paid for this, and now you're telling me we can't use it?' I had no good answer to that other than 'yes, that is what I'm telling you. I didn't tell you you had to buy it. You need to take it up with the people who did.' I think some of that is that some of the people who pushed the technology are not teachers. They see that as valuable but they aren't the ones who have to use it in the classroom. I love the bulletin board [WebCT], but I find the best use of it is outside class, in particular my graduate classes that don't meet very often.

Q: Speaking generally, what is the role of an academic library on a campus like ours?

A: First of all, there's an educational purpose. An educational purpose for faculty and students in terms of how to make good use of academic sources. The second thing is to make sure there's availability of the sources. And then what I really appreciate on a small campus like this is being able to go to you and say 'hey, I'm swamped right now, can you help me find this stuff quickly?' Its critical function is teaching people how to use the resources and making sure that the resources are there.

Q: How have libraries changed since you were in graduate school?

A: I think again the biggest change is that when I was in graduate school you went in and whatever resources were there were there. That was what was available. A librarian could assist you in finding resources in the library. I think the job is harder now, even though there may be fewer books. That's another comment I'd make about the technology. The other issue with the blessing and curse of the new technology is you have access to this unbelievable amount of information, so the librarian has to work harder to distinguish between good information and bad information. That's the biggest change – the sheer volume of information you have access to, and the ease with which you have access to it. But you still have to make some sense out of it.

Q: How important is collaborating with campus librarians to help your students learn research skills in your field?

A: I think it's crucial, both for undergraduates and for graduates. Our graduate students need almost as much help with their research skills as our undergraduates. The lack of research skills across the board is appalling. I don't see students getting enough help in learning how to research in the classroom from their regular teachers. I think the need to learn how to do research is more important than ever because they have access to so much information.

Q: With your current teaching load, how hard is it to conduct research and write papers?

A: It's very hard. Again, that's here, with our 4-4 load, no release time to speak of, committee work, etc. I think often the most committed teachers are the ones who get asked to do other things. With the amount of information that comes out in the literature of any field, it's very hard to stay up and very hard to do research.

Q: How different is your job as a college professor today from how you imagined it would be when you were in graduate school?

A: The difference is that you're always behind [laughs]. When I used to think of my teachers I assumed they spent a fair amount of time reading and writing, which they may well have done. But I find that I don't have that time. I'd love to go back to graduate school now and have a couple of years to learn. Right now I don't have enough time to keep learning to the depth that I would like to. Probably one of the reasons I went into teaching is that I like to learn. The assumption at times from the school is that when you become a teacher your basic learning is done.

Q: Can you describe any positive or negative experiences you've had with librarians in your career, both as a student and then as an instructor?

A: I have been consistently very impressed with the support I've received from librarians. When I've needed help it's been more than fully provided. The website here is very complete, informative and useful to its users. The quality of the help from the people here is what has struck me most, not whether or not we have every book. The emphasis needs to be there, in the service.

Q: Who should have primary responsibility for selecting books, videos, and journals in a college library – faculty, librarians, or some combination?

A: I would think a mix is best. It's hard for me to see how a librarian could know what are all the important journals in every field. So I think there would have to be consultation, with department faculty providing that kind of information. But the librarian has the big picture, the needs of the library as a whole, and that's where their expertise has to come in.

Q: Any other comments?

A: I would say that one of the challenges for librarians is how they stake their claim to be a full part of the faculty – and helping faculty see that role as legitimate. On the issue of tenure, for example, there are a number of different issues that would arise there. The challenge becomes: 'How do I claim full membership as a scholar and as an academician, even though I'm not relating to students the same way that someone in the classroom is?'

Mary Kay Jordan Fleming, Assistant Professor, Behavioral Sciences Department

Q: What are the major sources of stress in your job?

A: I'd say it's the competing demands for time. If you really want to do a good job teaching, you're constantly updating things, changing assignments. The committee work and advising is thrown in on top of that. E-mail has become so commonly used that it invades your time at home too, the feeling that you're on call 24 hours a day. That was not the case when I was first hired [1983].

Q: Can you estimate how many hours you work a week?

A: At least fifty. My time is divided up. I may leave my office earlier to do something with my kids, but then at night I might put in another four hours at home. Weekends are not sacred anymore either. Also, the faculty role in recruiting students did not exist until fairly recently. We're really expected to participate in almost everything. I see the need, but it's just another demand put on top of everything else.

Q: What are some common misconceptions that non-academics have about academics?

A: The single greatest one is that you're off in the summer. That's a complete myth. I've never found anybody – except another college faculty member – who understands that that is the case. What they don't realize is that if you do take the summer off, then you're not going to make progress on the things that get squeezed during the school year – scholarship, special projects, and new initiatives. The second misconception is that people think we have very cushy jobs because they see the flexibility we have within the daytime hours. If they see me come home at 2 o'clock they think, 'Isn't she lucky? She's off for the day!' I'm not. I'm going to work from six until ten, but they don't see that. The other misconception is that people think that teaching is 100 per cent of your job. They don't know about committee work. They tend not to know too much about the advising role. And they have no idea about the expectations for scholarship and service to the professional community.

Q: Can you break up by percentage the time you spend on teaching, doing research, doing committee work, etc.?

A: Well, I would have to say first of all that my way of dividing it up might be different from others. I am one of these compulsive over-preparers. There is one thing I will not do and that is walk in the classroom unprepared. I always have a plan B too. If we are planning on watching and discussing a video in class, I'll be prepared in case the video doesn't work. So I have mapped out three hours for every hour I'm teaching. Assuming I'm a full-time teacher, and I have only one committee assignment, I'd say something like 70 per cent teaching, 20 per cent committee work, and 10 per cent advising. Advising is episodic. When we have advising season going on, it will cut a three-week path out of your schedule. Then, at other times you're not investing in that. The committee assignments vary greatly too. I've been on some committees where there isn't that much time involved, but there are others that take up lots of your time.

Q: In your 70:20:10 breakdown, you didn't mention research and scholarship.

A: Good point. Realistically, make it 60:20:10:10. But that's August–May only. During June and July it's 90 per cent research. I know people who do the balance better, but I can't. I look for a lot of outside activities that involve kids, and I think that enriches my teaching. If I were a Chemistry teacher, I wouldn't say that, but I teach child development. I also teach lots of teachers. Since I don't have the classroom experiences they might, I bring in a lot of that other stuff as sources of examples. One thing enriches another. You're accountable to yourself. You have to do what your conscience tells you to do.

Q: Do you think your students use the library as much as they should?
A: No.

Q: Given that fact, who should get them to use the library more often, the professors or the librarians?

A: I think it has to be the faculty. Students don't stop by your office and say, 'Paul, do you think I ought to be in here more?' You have to press them. That's really the only way it's going to work. I would imagine that you participate in orientation, encourage them, send out periodic reminders, and advertise your services. But the faculty by structuring requirements in certain ways can – and we should. That's our responsibility. Having said that, the biggest thing that's made the difference is the Internet. I do not think the majority of students have any concept of the difference between refereed and non-refereed publications, or between the Internet and the library. And that is really disturbing at this level. The other thing that we're all facing is that students are coming into college with significant experience with the Internet from grade school and high school. That's where the bad habits start. I think they get bad habits in not recognizing the difference between quality and non-quality sources, and I think that they learn to be careless about copyright. Nobody's saying, 'You have to reword this, it's not okay to do this.' The concept of intellectual property with writing is hard to understand. Students now think they have all the same resources of a library at their command over a computer. They're picking up a lot of garbage and acting like it's equivalent to journal articles.

Q: Finish this sentence. I wish the library were …

A: Now it's going to sound like I'm as lazy as my students! I wish everything in the library were, in fact, available over the Internet, so you really could do it all from home.

Q: That's an understandable wish.

A: If cost were no object, that would make life simpler. Sometimes faculty availability doesn't match the access.

Q: Talk about your library experiences in general. Did any negative or positive experiences stay with you? Or, how has your use of the library changed since you were a graduate student?

A: Obviously the Internet things we've talked about have been the greatest change since I was in graduate school. It's changed the whole face of it. While I've been teaching, I'd say the biggest change has been in some of the mechanics of having to put articles on reserve, and some of the things that have been enormously simplified. Over the years I've also had a librarian come to my class and talk about how to do a particular assignment. That's a great service. My experiences with the library have been very good. It seems that if ever there has been a way to make things that were under your control simpler, then you have – requesting interlibrary loan articles, putting them in campus mail for me instead of having me walk over to get them. That sort of thing.

Q: What are the main things an aspiring academic librarian needs to know about the cultural climate on a small college campus?

A: I think one thing that I would hope they'd do is to do what you all do – to be full partners of the faculty. From committee work, to speaking up at meetings. You've done a good job of fully integrating it with teaching, but it might take a person who's aggressively pursuing that to do it. In other words, I could imagine a librarian who kind of hung back and thought 'when they need me, they'll visit.' I don't think you all do that and I don't think you should. Some new faculty might not come into the situation knowing that you're full partners, but here they will form that impression very quickly. So I would hope that librarians in training develop the mindset that they are full partners, that they deserve to be, and that they should look for opportunities to make that point to faculty.

Q: Can you walk me through your formal education, starting with your entry into graduate school?

A: First of all, I hope no one else would use my experiences as an example! My first major as an undergraduate was special education. Then, I fell in love with psychology and I decided to add that and graduated as a double major. I even did my student teaching in special education. But I thought I was going to be a good candidate for burnout in a couple of years. I tend to take on a lot emotionally and that's where the burnout comes in. So I thought maybe I should look into something else. I liked psychology well enough, but then I had a great professor in experimental psychology. He was a great teacher. That was the first time I thought there could be a career here. So I decided to go to graduate school right away. If I waited a couple of years and had a paycheck, I thought I would forget how to live on nothing. The longer you're out, the more commitments you get. So I went right to graduate school and that's where the trouble started. I did not like the faculty in my program. I thought they were not at all like me. I didn't get any support from them. I saw a bunch of people who had sacrificed their lives and their families for their careers, and I had no desire to do that. I didn't consider them as role models. But I did have one really good teacher whom I really admired, and that's why I stayed. Then, I became aware of a research assistantship at a local hospital and I snatched it. That became both my lifeline and my undoing because now I was off campus a lot, and that slowed me down. I knew what I was doing. I knew the choice that I was making. So it took me about three years to get my Master's. I was happy at the hospital and not in such a big hurry back on campus. It took me another seven years to finish graduate school. In between my Master's and my dissertation, I got married, built a house – luckily, we waited to have kids. I knew if I had kids I wouldn't finish. I had two big incentives for my final finishing. First, the provost here wrote it into my contract that I had to. I was here part-time in 1982, started full-time in 1983, and defended my dissertation in 1987. The other thing was that we wanted to have kids and I knew I wouldn't finish it once they were on the scene. I wasn't getting any younger! So I wanted to keep my job and I wanted to start a family.

Q: What are some adjectives or phrases that apply to a good college teacher?

A: In this environment I'd say that you need to be genuinely interested in student learning and have a commitment to that. You have to realize that although the students play the major role in that, there are things you can do, and that you have to be committed to doing them. One thing I feel very strongly about is being passionate about your discipline. If you're not, the students know it, and everyone in the room will be bored. But if your students know that you feel very strongly about this, and they get examples of how you use what you're teaching to make a difference in your life, that's very contagious.

Q: What are the changes you've seen in students since you first started teaching?

A: Their writing skills are worse. This is strictly conjecture – I have no data to support this – but I think they read less. That's just maddening. It directly affects my job. If I could say 'okay, you don't want to read, that's fine,' then the consequences would fall to them. But it's not that simple, because if they haven't read beforehand, then I can't do all the other interesting stuff that builds on it in class. I feel like I get sucked back in to reteaching the textbook, and I detest that! Another one is that these are students who are used to multitasking – a word I hate, but I can't think of an alternative – in every phase of their lives, and it drives me insane. They're used to hearing one thing and being entertained visually by something else at the same time. And you know, the world is not a sound byte. The media has trained us to think that everything can be said in one pithy sentence. And here you are, trying to develop their critical thinking skills – which involves reflectivity – while they're multitasking. People are getting more impulsive, which is something that can be very counterproductive.

Jack Hettinger, Associate Professor, Humanities Department

Q: What are the major sources of stress in your job?

A: Let's see. When I think of major sources of stress I think of eccentric and irrelevant things that the Dean does. Deans in general, that is. For example, the push to make all of our course objectives common. That's very foolish and ill-advised, and I don't think it's based on any research. It's based on an old behavioral sciences paradigm of having students clock in and drink at the trough. It's as if students can be conditioned to cognitively and effectively learn, and that if we do certain things to stimulate them they will learn. Really it's things that interfere with my vision of teaching. I want to teach students to think on their own about the subject matter, to understand the methodologies of discipline and critically challenge them. So this notion of uniform objectives seems to be an obstacle. The second thing that really gets on my nerves is how the students will see through this, how they'll see this as the same old kind of yadda yadda. Those who are so disposed will get even more cynical.

Q: What are some common misconceptions that people have about college professors?

A: Well, just gathering from comments in newspapers and on talk shows, that we don't do much work. The state legislatures want university professors to account for their hours in the same way that corporations want their employees to, as if we were some kind of machines working on producing something. Which is another source of tension for me, our industrial notion of education. In other words, if we follow uniform procedures and we stamp out the same model as it goes down the assembly line we will have done our job.

Q: Can you estimate how many hours a week you work during a typical semester?

A: Easily fifty, but I'm afraid it's a lot more. I find that in addition to working Monday through Friday I often work part of Saturday and Sunday. I often work after supper. My day will start with an 8 o'clock class in the morning and I usually get here well before that. It's kind of a scary question, because I don't want to think about it. That's a stressor too, because like everyone else I need a private life.

Q: Can you talk about the effect that technology has had on your teaching?

A: I use WebCT extensively. I have WebCT home pages for all of my courses. I have a lot of integral parts of the course located on WebCT, like links to articles, electronic reserves, the syllabus, and sometimes I'll put my lecture notes on there. I use laptops in the class all the time. I think until we bring in the human factor, we can say that all this is wonderful. As long as in my courses in literature the activity of the class is discussion, sharing and challenging of ideas, as long as all of these serve the socio-academic discussion it's wonderful. Students have not yet complained on my student ratings that the classroom use of the technology is overdone or replaces something else that is essential. They do complain – sometimes vociferously – about the discussion questions on WebCT. I've scaled back a little on that. The problem that I want to get to, though, is that I expect more of the students than they may realize they are capable of. I want to make sure that I make clear to them what the purposes of the technology are for their intellect. They aren't just pragmatic tricks. Technology can never be separated from the human personalities. It's the relationship that the teacher has with the students that is fundamental.

Q: You are married to a librarian. What are some of the things you've learned about librarianship from her?

A: The thing that I just did not fully realize is collection development. Even though academic departments are supposed to be responsible for making their own recommendations for the library, we rely on librarians to show us what's out there.

Q: Since books are so easily obtained via loan from OhioLINK, is it fair to say that you've recommended fewer books for our local collection?

A: Yes. I remember how your predecessor described the change, that we were moving into a borrowing environment.

Q: 'Access versus ownership' is one of the clichés in the profession.

A: Yes. At first since it was a brand new concept I didn't know how efficiently OhioLINK would operate. I was skeptical. I wasn't resistant, because we didn't have an economic choice. I'm delighted to see how well the system continues to work and improve.

Q: Do you think the students use OhioLINK as often as they might?

A: No, absolutely not. In the industrial model of education, where the student comes in to Dr. X's class, gets the drill, and leaves the class at the end of the semester with so many skills, then we're deluding ourselves if we think we're developing a critical student. When you use a teaching process that goes against this model, sometimes the students resist. They want you to get back to this model. They want certainty. If we give students too much certainty, then they don't think on their own. It's a combination of our failure to transcend this constricting process and the students' sense of discomfort inside of that process. To transcend that, you have to become your own knowledge maker, and to do that you have to get information, and to get information you have to do research, get a book from OhioLINK. It's up to us to demonstrate what this benefit is. There's a huge area for misunderstanding between students and teachers. Do teachers use OhioLINK enough? Do teachers integrate the ideas they've gained from OhioLINK resources enough?

Q: Is it the librarian's job to promote resources like OhioLINK to students, or is it the faculty member's job?

A: The faculty member's. We are the ones who have the closest relationship with the students. The student, for better or for worse, ultimately defers to our authority because we are the ones giving the grades. Again, it's this industrial model – grading students the way we do bonds. Somehow or other the students get educated in our educational system, but it's a mystery to me how. We need to be able to dwell on a subject with some degree of leisure, which is what school means – from the Greek term *scholi*, leisure to think, leisure to discuss. I would replace letter grades with narrative grades. These are hard things for Boards of Trustees to understand, though, most of whom are non-academics. Most of them think of college as skill development.

Q: What role should the library play on a college campus?

A: It should have one of the essential roles. It should be the place where we get information and ideas, the place that fuels our heresies and blasphemies. It doesn't have to be as dramatic as nailing theses to doors, but if we're going to continue to make new knowledge we have to teach people who can actually be critical of the process. That's a hard way to live your life. A good test to subject yourself to would be to read several good newspapers a day all the way through where you're getting analysis of critical national and international issues. It's a rough way to live, though, and a lot of us don't want to live that way.

Q: The examined life can drive one crazy, right?

A: I couldn't put it better. And then aside from looking at the world, looking at oneself.

Q: Have you had any particularly positive or negative experiences with libraries or librarians over the years?

A: No. The problems have only been external: limitations of funds or personnel.

Jeff Hillard, Associate Professor of English and Writer in Residence

Q: What are the major sources of stress in your job?

A: They would probably center on juggling time commitments between meetings, class demands, and professional needs, such as writing and publication. Stress comes from time management, which I'm not great at, being a creative person. I have to really work at getting things done on time, especially during the academic year.

Q: Can you estimate how a typical week is broken up by all your duties?

A: I'm starting my eighteenth year of teaching. I have tenure, so I've been able to reduce the time devoted to working on committees. Committees don't bother me as much as they used to. I was chair of a committee for a while. I'm glad to help when I can. Anyway, I'd say 60 per cent of my time goes toward teaching, 30 per cent toward writing, and 10 per cent goes to department meetings, committees, and avenues of community and college service. There are occasions when these percentages will change. I know how to teach, and I have great confidence in what I do prep-wise, so some years it will be 50 per cent teaching and 50 per cent writing. A great dream of mine would be to become a full-time writer, but I haven't got there yet. Now this 50:50 arrangement almost flies in the face of some colleagues who are ostensibly teachers only. I always find time for my writing.

Q: Including all the writing that you consider part of your job as a professor, how many hours a week do you estimate you work?

A: I'm constantly doing something. If it's not teaching or working on a class, it's working on a piece of writing. I'll say between 50 and 60 hours a week.

Q: I'm sure most people who work outside of the academy don't realize how many hours per week faculty members put in. What are some other major misconceptions they might have about faculty?

A: They think we're finished with work when our class is finished. We take work home all the time. I come from a background where, unfortunately I guess, my father's side is driven. I think I've got this gene. It's helped me and it's hurt me. In being driven I'll put a lot of chips in one particular project and will lose track of something else I'm supposed to be doing. That's where the stress comes in. I can deal with the students. I walk into a class very confidently that I can handle any situation. They don't give me stress the way they might with other faculty members. I'm a veteran at this. Although they're changing, the students are a lot of fun. A real misconception is that you're finished at 9 or 10 at night. Sometimes I write between 10 p.m. and 1 a.m.

Q: You mentioned some changes you've seen in your students. Can you go into detail about them?

A: A major change that I see right now is their anxiousness about everything. What I mean by that is often they get very impatient with things they need or want. They want you to cut right to the chase. Their attention spans are more limited than they used to be. The idea of the straight lecture is almost an anathema to them now. We used to have a lecture-oriented mode of teaching. The whole methodology has changed now to be more interactive with students. Also to be more interactive outside the class by using WebCT. I've seen a generation of students coming through now that is more demanding of our expertise. They want their information and then they want to fly. They don't want it fifty minutes after the class starts; they want it ten minutes after the class starts. If you don't deliver, or you don't catch what they need, they'll turn you off. The students become even hungrier for information as the semester goes on.

Q: What do you think a would-be academic librarian needs to know about the academic culture to succeed in this field?

A: I'd say that they need to be well equipped with all kinds of modes of presentation – the computers, the hands-on help, and the research help. I can't tell you how many times the librarians here have really come to bat for students who've needed a helping hand in doing their research. I think in the future I envision a part of the library having a neon light saying 'research help' here, as opposed to being just a place that has books. There will be a more proactive approach. In 18 years here I've never been hesitant to tell one of my students to go over to the library and get help. I know that our library staff are good enough and that they care enough to get the students what they need. Our library here is one where I don't just think about the books. They help greatly with student and faculty research, and I see this role expanding even more in the future.

Q: Do your students use the library enough?

A: Yes and no. I don't think they use the library as much on their own accord. They need to be nurtured to use it. If I've let them know that certain poetry books are there, or certain journals are there, then they'll come over and not gripe about it. They end up finding something that they didn't think they would and that pleases them. You have to lay that groundwork.

Q: Why did you decide to get your MFA and why did you decide to become a teacher at the college level?

A: I knew I was going to write before I felt I was going to become a college professor. I knew I was going to be a writer in some capacity by the time I was 16. When I was a college senior I was working for a newspaper, but I didn't care for my boss. I wasn't sure what to do at that point. My family is a family of teachers, so I took another year and a half to get my teaching certificate. I taught high school for half a year and then decided to go west because I wanted to go further in teaching. I thought if I got an MA in creative writing I could teach at a community college. I was in Boulder [Colorado] for three and a half years because I could only afford to take one or two classes per term. I was writing for a newspaper and I also delivered pizzas when I wasn't in class. I also edited ad copy for about six months. My wife worked full-time. She was shouldering most of the load at that time. I knew that writing and getting published was important to me even at the age of 23 when I went west to Boulder. I started to publish in literary journals when I was 20 or 21. I established a good track record early in my twenties. One of the reasons I was hired here in 1987 was that the Humanities department chair at the time recognized my name from some local publications. That helped our conversation progress and it helped open the door to this job.

Q: Did the Mount have a writer in residence before you came?

A: Yes, I replaced Nikki Giovanni. She taught here from 1979 to 1986 at the request of Sr. Jean Patrice Harrington, the Mount's president at the time. It was almost like a favor. They were good friends. In 1986, Sr. Jean Patrice resigned and so did Nikki. That left the position open. I got lucky. You have to get lucky in these situations. I'd literally walked over here the week after graduation and started a conversation with the department chair I referred to earlier.

Q: Complete this sentence. I wish the campus library were ...

A: I wish it would be given a great deal of room and leverage within the institution and by the administration to work the magic that it can work. I wish it could become more of a campus center, that some work could be done cosmetically to the interior. I wish it was also empowered to utilize faculty and staff in all kinds of literary activities, like readings, or even music. Round table discussions – those kinds of things – on a bi-weekly basis. Don't worry about who comes, don't worry about affecting schedules, just do it, just offer it and see what happens. Our library would be the perfect place for activities like this.

Q: How different is your job from how you imagined it might be when you were in graduate school?

A: I thought the administration at the College would recognize better how faculty spend their time. I feel like there should be a great deal more flexibility in the way that classes are scheduled vis-à-vis the talents and skills the professors bring to the college. In some sense the College has been very giving in letting writers come on campus, but if I were given a reduced load of say three classes a term, I'd hope they could allow me to use the time I'd normally take to teach a fourth class to instead create a series of literary or intellectual activities on campus. I'd jump at the chance. I've been here long enough that I feel I should be in a negotiable position on issues like this. This college is about image, it's about making sure its name is out there so that it can attract students. Discussions like these would make it more attractive. Could taking time to arrange these events be considered part of my load? Could it replace the time I'd otherwise spend on a committee? I can't do all this and teach four classes and keep up my writing at the same time. There has to be some incentive. You can't bleed a professor dry. That's why a lot of small colleges are stepping stones for faculty to go on to larger universities where their teaching load is reduced. Look at how companies are changing. They're recognizing the individual talents of their employees. They're giving them more liberty to do those things they do especially well. You used to sit in your seat, take orders from the top, and the product is produced. Now companies are realizing that good leadership comes when leaders allow their people more room and flexibility. I don't feel that many professors here have comparable opportunities. One of the reasons I don't go out of my way anymore to bring in writers is that I'm not recognized for such efforts.

Q: What makes a good academic librarian?

A: You have to be people-friendly and a good communicator about what the library can offer, what new resources it has. I think a challenge for librarians is to demystify the old notion of a library as hallowed ground. You want this image to remain in some ways, but you want to create an image of a library as more user-friendly than it has been in the past.

Shirley Hoenigman, Assistant Professor of Chemistry

Q: What are the major sources of stress in your job?

A: Trying to get everything done. As a junior faculty member, I have the tenure anvil hanging over my head, so it's hard to try to find the appropriate balance between teaching, scholarship, and academic citizenship. That's been a constant struggle. Philosophically, it's been hard to accept from the institution that those are the three areas I need to be equally proficient in.

Q: Can you estimate the percentage of your time you spend on all these activities?

A: According to our brochure, it should be one third to each of them, but that's not the case. As far as my teaching responsibilities are concerned, it varies from semester to semester depending on how much prep time I need, but probably about half of my time is devoted to that. I'd say 30–35 per cent is devoted to citizenship and the rest to scholarship.

Q: Do you think too much of your time is spent on citizenship?

A: I came to the Mount at a time of great change. We've done curriculum reform, we've gone through higher learning commission, and so the demands on citizenship are such that you can't always say no. I feel like the responsibility to take on these needs is always coming at the expense of scholarship. Teaching is the one place that you can't drop the ball, so that's the place I tenaciously make sure those things are getting done as they should be getting done. So other things get sacrificed in the name of that. I certainly feel tension in the citizenship arena from the standpoint that some of the citizenship things I want to do, I can't. I have to do these other things. I try to console myself with the fact that I only have to put up with this for a finite number of years.

Q: So the reality of the job hasn't always met your expectations?

A: The Mount hasn't matched them. I had another job at an institution where they used more of a two out of three approach. It was still the same expectation in those areas but not weighted equally. They thought a little bit more broadly about what constitutes scholarship. The Mount is a little bit more rigid in their definition of those things. Realistically, the goal is to present the airtight case to Promotion and Tenure, but if you're going to do that it comes at a price.

Q: Do your students use the library enough? And if they aren't, whose responsibility is it to get them to use it more?

A: Everybody's got a role in that. A lot of my teaching in my discipline is upper level, so by the nature of the content students should be relying increasingly on the scientific literature, not on the textbook. I constantly try to force them to go to the literature to find this value, or to find certain things. As far as them physically coming over to the library, I don't know how often that happens. In one of my classes I brought some issues of a journal that I personally subscribe to and plopped them down on their desks, saying 'would you please read some of these!?' I reminded them that most articles like this are online, but they said it was easier if I just gave it to them. So there's student culpability to be sure. I don't know of any faculty member who doesn't feel like they're constantly competing for the students' attention. I also think that every faculty member feels the pressure to get through the content that you have to get through, and you simply can't, short of requiring about six more classes. I'm especially concerned about the lack of research from students who want to go to graduate school. It's less of a concern, I suppose, for those who want to go straight into industry.

Q: Have you used library instruction to help address this?

A: Yes, we started the Chemistry Seminar course in which a librarian gave a talk, so with luck I'll be the beneficiary of this in the future. When I've taught the IDS 100 course [a required course for all freshmen] we show them how to find the goldmine of information, but from their point of view it still takes too long. I find that there's a threshold. If they can't find what they need in five minutes, then they think it's not there.

Q: Is the library meeting your needs? The needs of a junior faculty member?

A: So far so good, but I'm about to really run up against a solid answer to that pretty soon. I need to start doing the background information for an interdisciplinary paper, and at this point I'm a little bit nervous, simply because the interdisciplinary literature is a body of literature I'm not that familiar with. I don't know what the best resources are in that area. By and large in my own discipline I can get the journals I need through OhioLINK. If there are any second-tier analytical chemistry journals I can get that at UC [University of Cincinnati]. It's not an accident that I end up teaching at places that have a large institution nearby where I can get hardcopies if I don't want to wait. I've found the databases pretty cooperative to search. There's always a little twitch in the back of my brain – since I did my doctorate at the University of Michigan, where you get spoiled – so I'm always wondering if I really got everything on the topic.

Q: Can you explain the pressures you feel going up for tenure?

A: It depends on the day of the week. Most of the time my reality is that if I don't get tenure here, then I'll get another job. I'm marketable, I'll be okay. There are days when I'm not sure if I even want to go through the tenure process here. I'll feel the tension more on those days I feel that this is really where I want to stay. I don't feel like my entire career is hinged on this decision. I can always pick up and leave. I've done it before and I can do it again. I try to keep things in perspective. The memos that you get from your pre-tenure review say clearly 'these are the things you need to do'. It's dictated to you, and like any academic, I don't like to be told what to do! [Laughs.] That's where I'll feel pressure. You're not most effective when you're doing something because you *have* to do it. There are pressures with scholarship. When it needs to be done, when it needs to appear in print, who the audience needs to be, who is appropriate to review it – those kinds of things do bother me more. I don't always have the best sense of what it is they're looking for.

Q: When you were in graduate school did you know that you eventually wanted to teach at a small institution, as opposed to a large university?

A: I started trying to feel out where I wanted to be in my fourth year of grad school. We usually take about five years in my camp to finish up. I went through a lot of industrial interviews, thinking that if I could find my dream industrial job, I'd take it. I never did. So it was only then that I seriously started to think about teaching. I really thought long and hard about what that would mean. In my discipline, if you choose to go the small college route, you close doors behind you. I had to make sure that that would be a choice I would be okay with. I thought about that for a very long time. My background had nothing to do with small colleges. Both of my institutions had 30,000 plus people. I really didn't have any experience with it at all. The more I thought about it, and the more I thought about my teaching experience in graduate school, I thought it was a better fit for the things I care about and how I want to spend my time. So I jumped in.

Q: Have the students here surprised you – in good and bad ways?

A: I've had a lot of major disappointments in the classroom, as far as capability is concerned. Again, I came here from another small place that wasn't prestigious, so I thought at least it would be a parallel move. I found that a lot of chemistry terms I thought I could use with a junior level class were not understood. I took it for granted that they knew what I was talking about. At the same time I've had some students who have absolutely blossomed. Sometimes you do see the curiosity blossom, and you do see the motivation there, the hunger. I'm starting to get to the point now where students are coming back and telling me 'wow, now I get what you were talking about!' One student has e-mailed me four times this summer, absolutely doing cartwheels and thanking me for what I taught her the previous year.

Q: What are some common misconceptions that non-academics have about academics?

A: That we get the summers off!

Q: Can you describe how you spend your summers?

A: It varies from summer to summer – at least for me. This last summer was pretty intense on research because I got some grant money. I'm also doing collaboration with a colleague in Missouri. And I felt I had more time to do scholarship this summer than I have previously here. The summer before I spent developing the IDS 100 course [a required course for all freshmen]. It was a huge amount of work! On the one hand, that's to your benefit because it's fun and you get to do some innovative things in the classroom. On the other hand, you also hear this little voice saying 'that's not going to help you get tenure.' To get back to your question about how academics are perceived, it's different for me. All I have to do is say 'chemistry' and I get one of three answers. One: 'you must be really smart!' Two: 'you must like math!' Or three: 'ooh, I hate chemistry. That's my worst class!' I could be a chemist digging a ditch and I'd get the same answer. The academic part of it is irrelevant.

Q: You did your graduate work at the University of Michigan, so you had tremendous library resources at hand. How much of a substitute for this has OhioLINK with all of its resources been?

A: So far it has been. In my discipline there's a pretty standard set of journals that we use and publish in. I've found that I've had access to all of these without too much difficulty. I did maintain my personal subscription to *Analytical Chemistry* up until about a year ago, because I was satisfied with OhioLINK.

Q: When you came here for your interview, did you ask questions about the library collection?

A: Yes, absolutely. When I was considering applying here, I really did a lot of work to check this place out. I already had the list of journals they subscribed to here at the time, I think. At that time they were awaiting news from the American Chemical Society to see if the program would be accredited. That said, I knew they had to have all the required journals. Compared to the small school I'd taught at previously – where the library was massively deficient – the access here was very, very nice. I do remember getting a tour of campus and going by the Chemical Abstracts. I was really impressed by that. Also, I knew UC was nearby.

Q: Complete this sentence. I wish the campus library were ...

A: Hm. I guess I don't feel there's anything else the library would do. I wish the students would go to the library more. I feel like the library has been very helpful.

Q: Do you think the students come to college with poor library habits? Do students all over the country avoid going to the library, or is it just our students here?

A: That's a good question. The attitude they have is that they want a 20-minute rationale for everything. When I was an undergraduate, it was 'I don't know when I'm going to have to know this, but he's telling me I'm going to have to know this someday, so I'd better do it.' Perhaps it was just a different way of looking at faculty. There's a disconnect. Even when you do give them the rationale, they don't always internalize it. I'm one of the youngest faculty members on campus, but even my high-school experience is utterly irrelevant to understanding our students. They don't rely on physically going to the library and physically getting a book because they grew up with the Internet. One of my students didn't even know how to use the index of a book! So I don't know what the answer is.

Sue Johnson, Associate Professor, Health Sciences Department

Q: What are the major sources of stress in your job?

A: Student complaints and concerns about the program, or grade appeals, and things like that. Workload, in that there's too much to do and not enough time to do it in. Since I'm a program director, there are many administrative duties that have to be completed by certain dead-lines. Sometimes I wish there would be more help from ancillary staff who could do the administrative things when we could be focusing more on curriculum and course development. Often it's just the unexpected student concerns that pop up.

Q: What about scholarship? Is that stressful?

A: Most of my writing and scholarship takes place on the weekend at home. That's just another added piece. Being tenured, I still feel the need to continue to do that because of post-tenure review. Plus there's the desire to do that. It's hard to work it in during a normal work day. There are no interruptions at home. I'm the type of person who needs long blocks of time to work.

Q: Can you take me through your experience with getting tenure?

A: For me it was a long haul. When I first came to the Mount I didn't have a PhD. While I still had a full teaching load I had to complete my doctoral course work and my dissertation. I did take one year off where I only taught part-time in order to finish my doctoral course work. It's not easy, plus I had two small children at home, but it can be done. On the road to tenure you have to show your community service. I got hooked up with a coalition in Covington, Kentucky that dealt with pregnant teenagers, and that organization provided me with the data for my dissertation, 'Outcomes of Teen Pregnancy.' So I tried to blend what I was doing on campus with what I was doing for the doctoral work. That made it workable for me. I finished the doctoral dissertation in 1998.

Q: What was your deadline for applying for tenure?

A: Let's see. I think they put me on the tenure track after I finished my doctoral dissertation. The Dean gave me three years after I finished the dissertation to develop more scholarship. And she was right. It was worth the extra time because I got a couple of more articles published. I started here in 1992 and I got tenure in 2001. The pre-tenure review process was very helpful and my department chair gave me some very good guidance, too. I made a few mistakes in the pre-tenure process. I had a couple of colleagues look at my portfolio before I turned it in. The main stress was thinking 'if I don't get tenure I'm losing my job.' If you're ready and you've done the right things, though, it's just a matter of putting it together.

Q: What are some common misconceptions about faculty members?

A: I can tell you that in nursing there's a saying that goes: 'if you can't nurse, teach.' This is just horrible. It doesn't make any sense. How can you teach if you can't do it yourself? You hear people say that we have easy schedules, and we make a lot of money, and we can come and go as we please. Of course I don't agree with that. Some of them also think that we know everything.

Q: Why did you decide to become a nursing professor rather than a practising nurse?

A: When I decided to be a nurse I wanted to be a bedside nurse. I was in nursing school for about six months, in the associate degree program, and I met a faculty member whom I really admired. I remember thinking 'that's what I want to do.' It just took me a while to get there, because first I had to finish the associate degree, then the baccalaureate degree, and in the process I had two children. I entered the BSN to PhD program at the University of Cincinnati, because I already had a Master's degree in Psychology. Nursing was my second life.

Q: So you received a bachelor's and Master's degree in Psychology first? And then you went back at the associate level for nursing?

A: Yes. I thought I wanted to become a bedside nurse. I was sick of school and that was the fastest way to do it. I worked for two years as a bedside nurse on a Med-Surg floor and then six years in Labor-Delivery. A big factor was also that my husband was a faculty member. The life in academia appealed to me. You were always learning something new. It seemed like a great opportunity. I thought the stress would be lower than in bedside nursing! So I had some misconceptions about the faculty life too. The students are also much different than they were when I first started teaching in 1992. They do not seem to be quite as hungry for knowledge. They seem to have the attitude that they're here so they can get jobs as opposed to learning nursing as a career. They want all the information given to them. 'What's going to be on the test?' they ask. I enjoy teaching, but it's not quite as fun as I imagined it might be. You have to try to get them interested and excited about the content.

Q: How important is collaborating with librarians in helping your students learn research skills?

A: I think that it's very important. In fact, I was even hoping that the library could offer some kind of Informatics course. When I was working on my dissertation the library here was very helpful in getting me what I needed. I think you even mailed some articles to my house so I didn't have to come on to campus to get them!

Q: What kind of strategies have you used to teach your students library skills?

A: This summer was the first time we've actually had a librarian come and talk to students. Sometimes I'll help students on an individual basis in my office, help them pull up articles on CINAHL. We encourage them to go to the library and ask a librarian to help them if they can't find what they need. Some of them don't do that. Or they don't come in early enough to request the articles they need by interlibrary loan.

Q: When you see the students in the junior level courses you teach, how many of them are what we would call information literate – being able to find and evaluate information for their course needs?

A: I would say only half.

Q: Are there any positive or negative library experiences you can describe?

A: Probably the worst library was one where nobody would help me. They wouldn't know the answers to my questions. They couldn't help me with CINAHL searches. There was one librarian there who knew everything and the rest just didn't know.

Q: Were the people who couldn't help you professional librarians with Master's degrees, or some other personnel?

A: I think they were support help. There was one main librarian, but she didn't sit at the Reference Desk very often.

Q: Who should have responsibility for selecting materials for the library collection, faculty, librarians, or some combination?

A: Probably some combination. Faculty should recommend items, but you should have the final say. You have access to lists like the Brandon-Hall list [an annual list of best titles in nursing and related fields], and that's very helpful. You make sure the library collection stays where it needs to stay to remain a respected library. It's done well here. Everything we've asked for here we've gotten. I wouldn't want the main responsibility of making sure that the collection was up to date.

Q: Finish this sentence: I wish the library ...

A: I wish the library would offer an Informatics course.

Q: Would you require it for your students?

A: Yes, especially if we could have some input on it. Other than that, I wish the library would continue doing what it's doing because it works for me.

Q: What characteristics does a successful professor have? What adjectives apply to good professors?

A: They need to be current, innovative, creative, and flexible. They need to be good listeners, have high expectations for students and be able to hold to those. They need to be honest and ethical, intelligent, ambitious, and persistent.

Q: What have you learned from your students?

A: If there's one thing they've taught me it is that there is no black and white in nursing. They have forced me to look at things differently. Since I've been here I've done a complete turnaround in the way I teach. I started off teaching the way I was taught – by lecture. Now I lecture twenty minutes to get the class going, then it's group activities, case studies, going over visual aids. I use PowerPoint, because I've learned that just because it's said, it's not learned. You have to try to be sensitive to the way people learn.

Q: Any final thoughts?

A: Sometimes I think faculty don't use the library enough. We're not over here enough unless we're working on a particular project. One time

I walked over here to get something and saw one of my students. She said, 'what are you doing here?'

Q: Yes, they say faculty need to model behavior like this – that is, using the library – if they expect their students to do the same.

A: Yes, that's true.

Mike Klabunde, Assistant Professor of Classics

Q: What are some common misconceptions that you think non-academics have about college professors?

A: The most common thing is the idea that we have summers off. That we have really cushy, very well paid jobs, and that we're elitist. I also think they have this notion that we're aloof and detached from reality, this notion of the Ivory Tower – which, as we all know, comes from Lucretius, but I digress. It's become so clear to me over the last few years how much of what we teach isn't academic, it's attitudes and mindsets. It's not as glamorous as some people might think and it certainly isn't cushy.

Q: What are some of the major sources of stress in your job?

A: Scholarship is a major source of stress. The focus on really good teaching has been totally lost here. Something has to be juggled. I think our three categories for promotion and tenure (scholarship, teaching, and academic citizenship) have to be weighted completely differently with teaching absolutely paramount, then academic citizenship, and probably scholarship last.

Q: When people apply to a college like ours, do you think they expect that so much scholarship will be expected of them?

A: The search committees I've been on have always concentrated on teaching, teaching, teaching. Research was talked about, but it was really very much in the background. I think they come to a small place like this because they want to teach and have smaller classes.

Q: Can you walk me through your formal education?

A: As soon as I graduated with my bachelor's I came to Cincinnati to start the Master's and eventually the PhD program. After three years I had finished the Master's stuff but not gotten the Master's. They said 'you're doing well, so we'll waive all this, and you can start in on the doctoral work.' But I got sidetracked. I was young, I fell in love for the first time, and I was burned out. I was basically ABD [all but the dissertation], but not officially because I hadn't taken the comps [comprehensive examinations]. From 1978 to 1994 I didn't do the degree stuff. In 1984 I did something called the RSA Dip [Royal Society of Arts Diploma Program] in teaching English as a foreign language to adults. It was a distance learning program. I had to go to London, which was fun. Again, I did the work, but didn't ever go back to London to take the final examination. I didn't have the money to do it. In 1994 I started to go back, part-time, in Classics. The carrot was that the Dean told me she would put me in a tenure track position once I'd passed my comps and had my dissertation proposal accepted. So I got my Master's in 1999, took my comps in 2000, and wrote the dissertation in a year. I was the first one there [University of Cincinnati] in 20 years to finish a PhD in Philology. It's just murder.

Q: How important is collaborating with campus librarians in helping your students learn research skills?

A: Very important. They think everything is online. The library is there to give students and faculty information access. To me, the library is a cathedral, a holy space. It's the repository of humanity! The fact that much of that is now digital just astounds me. What I hear from the students here is that the library doesn't have what they want. Which I think back before OhioLINK might have been true. Now, though, I don't buy that excuse. Students are sometimes astounded when I tell them about OhioLINK. That's one thing I really want to get into IDS 100 [a required course for all freshmen]. Susan Falgner did some excellent presentations for that class last year.

Q: When the students are ignorant of something like OhioLINK, whose responsibility is it to educate them?

A: It's a shared endeavor. First it has to come from faculty. The faculty member has to model this desired behavior. Then the library staff, any chance they can, have to get the word out. The biggest misconception about the library is that it's this big, separate place that you go to as a last resort. Whereas it should be the place to start.

Q: Have you had any positive or negative experiences with libraries or librarians over the years?

A: Very positive ones. I've always thought librarians to be some of the most helpful people. Two of the librarians at the UC Classics library I thanked in my dissertation. One of the librarians there was positively maternal in how she acted towards me. Here, at the Mount, you have been astounding. Susan Falgner has been fabulous too. But really whoever is sitting at the Reference Desk has always been very helpful.

Q: How hard is it to conduct research and do scholarship with your teaching load and other duties? How are you managing to find time to work on your book?

A: Summer is a downtime. Our Dean has also been absolutely supportive. She basically said, 'go home this summer and write your book.' I'm on a 12-month contract, too, so where I'd normally be here in the office, I'm home. My Chair has been very supportive. I'm in a field that doesn't change tremendously fast either. For me, it's turning out to be just a lot of self-discipline.

Q: Finish this statement. I wish the library ...

A: ... played a larger role in the students' lives.

Q: Why do you think it doesn't?

A: I wish the students would view this place more like I do, as a cathedral of knowledge. They perceive it more as a specific place you have to go to as a last resort. I wish they would just wander the stacks, pull a book off a shelf, and just read. One of my colleagues says that today's students aren't in love with learning. They just want credentialing. That, frankly, is the history of the US educational system. I don't know how to make it a happening place. Their mindset is 'if I can't find it online I guess I have to go to the library.' The reverse would be a better notion.

Tim Lynch, Professor of History

Q: What are the major sources of stress in your job?

A: For me, even though I'm at a small college, I'd say class size. In history, where you want the students to write, it takes a lot of time to grade papers, especially here where we pitch ourselves as the 'Cheers' of higher education, where everybody knows your name. It's a stress to provide this kind of academic attention – in respect to grading papers – when typically my classes close at around 30 students. The average here is about 14. Another source of stress is that a significant portion of our students are not as prepared as I would hope. This makes the grading of all those papers that much harder. In the last five years, the percentage of our incoming freshmen that have satisfied all four criteria for admission has gone from 75 per cent down to 56 per cent. So only half of our students satisfy all four criteria. That's another source of stress. You want to challenge all the students, yet they're at many different places. It's very difficult to have students who would shine anywhere and then you have other students who have difficulty in understanding basic concepts. You can't get angry at the students, because we let them in the door. Maybe I'm romanticizing my past, but I think what the average undergraduate is capable of today is different than it was 30 years ago when I left college. A growing portion of our students have learning disabilities as well. Most who come the longest distance to the Mount are those who are Excel students. [Project EXCEL is a comprehensive academic support program at the College designed for students with specific learning disabilities who are enrolled in the traditional college curriculum.] They're better off being here, but when you put them together with the other students it is a challenge.

Q: Can you take me through your academic career, starting with after you had received your bachelor's?

A: I went right from high school to Xavier University, where I majored in Philosophy and History. Typical of people my age back then, there was less of an interest to choose a degree that pointed you towards a career. There was almost an embrace of that which could not be commercialized. I was going to go to graduate school at Boston College. I was there for two weeks in American Studies, but then the monies coming from the federal government that I'd hoped would support me went to the undergraduates. When it was clear that I didn't have the financial resources I dropped out, lived in Boston for one year, moved back to Cincinnati and got a job as an audiovisual technician at Xavier. That allowed me to get the credentials to be certified to teach high school. I took advantage of their tuition remission. After one year of working at Xavier there was an opening at LaSalle High School. They ran me out of the classroom. I was very young looking. One of the other teachers told me that 'this was the worst group of bad actors ever assembled in one classroom.' By January it was pretty clear that I needed to sever my ties with LaSalle if I was going to ever have any interest in teaching again. I was able to leave in January and they let me use that time to satisfy my student teaching requirement. I spent what would have been the second semester working as a carpenter. I was really ready to give up teaching altogether because that experience had left such a bad taste in my mouth. There was an opening at Brown County Ursuline where there were only 56 students. The students were very motivated. I came into my own there. It wasn't combat in the classroom any more. I didn't make any money, but it was a wonderful experience. After two years they closed. I had the opportunity while at Brown County to teach a little at Chatfield College. That gave me a taste of college teaching, but I certainly wasn't ready at that point to go beyond teaching high school.

I taught at Covington Catholic after Brown County Ursuline closed and spent seven years there. While I was there I began working part-time on a Master's degree in Humanities. It was during the summers and there was one semester that I had a reduced load. This was not a program billed as a stepping-stone program for a PhD. There was no language requirement, it was only in one discipline, and there was not a thesis per se that was required. I got that degree in 1988, after four years. Actually I had most of the coursework done by two years, but there was a project that took me longer to finish. Inertia set in. I pushed it to one side for a time. About that time I was also getting anxious for a change. I went to Highlands High School and taught there one year. I realized then that I wasn't just looking for a change of venue, but a different challenge. I decided at that point to get a PhD at Miami University. As I think of it, it was one of those really critical decisions in my life that was based very little on reality. I was married, we already had a home, and we wanted to stay in the Cincinnati area. I was also looking forward to being a student again. I wasn't thinking that much of the job market at the time. After two years I did my residency and there was an opening here at the Mount. I really wasn't ready to put myself on the market, but here was a job in American Social History in my backyard and certainly I wanted to apply for it. As I look back on it I was extremely lucky because I've since been told that there were 70 or 80 other applicants. I shared an office at Miami with another one of the applicants! I took my candidacy exams the first year I was here at the Mount. Technically, I wasn't even ABD [all but the dissertation]. I finished the PhD four years later. My advisor was wonderful throughout the whole process. I didn't have to start from scratch on my dissertation topic. They let me incorporate my interest in labor music along the way. My department chair was also wonderful. He never put pressure on me. I never felt pressure from the administration either, although I know some others in my situation did.

Q: How different was it for you to teach college students as opposed to high-school students? Did it meet your expectations?

A: My very first semester here I realized that the students were not familiar with many things I assumed would be basic knowledge, like how the constitution is amended. I presumed knowledge on the part of students that they didn't have. Of course there are a lot of perks to teaching at the college level. You're not *in loco parentis*. There's a different atmosphere. You don't have to deal with a lot of the silliness that you have to in high school. Anyway, I pretty quickly regrouped. I found out what they did know and went from there.

Q: What are some common misconceptions that non-academics have about those who teach at the college level?

A: I constantly hear from family about the whole schedule business. I read an article that said, according to the Bureau of Labor Statistics, that college professors and airline pilots had the highest wages per hour. The source of this misconception is that they think the only time that you're working is in the classroom. I don't think people often understand the kinds of pressure that we're under. Will that article get accepted? Can I get tenure? For every person who lands a job there are scores of others who could do the job equally well.

Q: How many hours a week do you work on average?

A: I'd guess between 50 and 60 hours. What's different about those hours is that you have a great deal of flexibility. With the computers now you can often do a lot of what you need to do from different places. Getting back to the misconceptions, members of my family would ask 'Are you finished with that paper yet?' referring to my dissertation as if it were a term paper you crank out in one night. Students are also often blind to the other duties professors have. The 1940s image of the college professor as this guy with a pipe and a tweed jacket with patches on the elbow has been perpetuated. That he sits around his office all day and has great thoughts.

Q: What are the key elements of a good working relationship between faculty members and librarians?

A: It's getting increasingly important to have a good relationship because the tools by which students gather information are changing so quickly. When I started my graduate education it was still sitting on those bar stools in the library with card catalog drawers, writing down call numbers. Just going to the computerized catalog was a huge step and that was just doing the same thing a different way. Now with all the search engines, the full text has changed everything. My way of approaching my research has changed. If you don't have a good relationship with librarians, or if you don't put your students in contact with librarians to learn the tools then they will never learn them. Unfortunately, they'll take the line of least resistance. They'll do their research by getting on Google. You try to tell the students that if they learn the good tools it will really save them time. The tools are constantly changing, which makes it even more important. I always bring in a librarian to talk to my class when I teach my senior research course. Lots of historical sources have not been digitized, so it's important for them to learn that just bringing up things on a screen is not enough. They've always had the Internet; they've always had this immediacy, so it's hard for them to learn that lots of research is grunt work. I don't care how good your search engines are, there's a lot of time spent doing grunt work. I lean on librarians all the time. You wouldn't have been mentioned in the acknowledgement of my book if I didn't!

Q: Since it's so easy to get books delivered to our library via Ohio-LINK have you recommended fewer books for our local collection?

A: Yes and no. Actually, let me turn the question around a little. What we expect as teachers is that, given any topic students choose, they'll be able to winnow through what's available and choose the most important ones. With OhioLINK it's easy to tell students, 'Hey, the books are out there. They may not be in our library, but they're easy to get.' They're not on our shelves, but they will be on that little shelf behind the circulation desk in a few days.

Q: Do students do their research long enough in advance to be able to wait for 2–4 days for their books to come from an OhioLINK school?

A: It depends on the student. Lots of them will put themselves behind the eight ball with OhioLINK and everything else by lying around the dorm for the first eight weeks of the semester. If they take it seriously, yes, they'll do it.

Q: With all these resources available, is it the responsibility of the professors or the librarians to make students aware of them?

A: I think it's a combination. If a student is writing a paper on the anniversary of the Lewis and Clark expedition, for example, I can tell them which books would be good. I can put that expectation on students. Now, how to get this source, that's where I rely on the librarian. I know that the librarians have the ability to get what the students need.

Q: How important is the library to your academic well-being?

A: It's essential, in a lot of different ways. One reason is just to have a place where you can go and not be disturbed. I've sought out the library on evenings when I still have a handful of papers to grade before that night's class. When I go to the library I know I can escape the telephone, the computer, the knock on the door, all the other distractions that occur in the office. As far as the resources go, well it's absolutely essential, and the librarians here have been wonderful.

Q: What does the future hold for libraries? How will they be different in twenty years?

A: You're asking a historian?! We have trouble in understanding the past, let alone predicting the future! I presume that much of what has occurred in the last decade with respect to the sources going online will mean that the library's ability to meet the needs of students and faculty will not be tied to what's on the shelf physically. Don't get me wrong, there will always be a place for books and journals on the shelf, but I can't imagine that being a library's top priority. The tools of research changed very little when I was a student, but now these tools are changing so often and so fast that students will need to learn more and more about how to use a library from librarians.

Q: Are there any downsides to these technological changes?

A: Well, when there was a card catalog, what was there to teach? You find the author's last name, title of the book, or subject area. That could just as easily be muttered by a professor in the classroom as by a librarian. There's a divide now between what professors know and what the new library resources are. I don't necessarily mean this in a bad way, but there is a divide. Professors do themselves a disservice if they presume they know all the ways in which information is available, and they also do their students a terrible disservice if they pretend they can tell their students all the ways in which they can do their research. In my research class I have a librarian sign off to indicate that the student has done everything that a librarian would have them do. This helps me, too, because I don't have to replicate all the steps of research to make sure that they have done what they should.

Q: Finish this sentence. I wish the library were ...

A: Better funded.

Q: Amen!

A: Our status as an institution has recently changed from 2B to 2A. That means that our institution is now putting greater emphasis on graduate programs. This puts us in the same category as the University of Dayton and Xavier University. To support graduate programs well, a library has to have many more resources than to support undergraduate programs. How many books does a library have, how many journals? These are the things that accrediting agencies want to know, and for a good reason! It's going to be a real tension here. In some ways it's no different than what it costs to hire faculty to teach in these programs.

Peg McPeak, Chair, Humanities Department

Q: What are the major sources of stress in your job?

A: I would say the fact that students find their information in other ways than through the print media. Much of what we do in the area of humanities depends on them being able to read and understand what they read. I think the stress comes there because they can't read, because they don't. They're not used to finding information in the print media. You're also trying to have them be active learners. Well, if they can't start with the idea and understand it, then having them do something, in terms of seeing its relevance, is very difficult. So we end up having to tell them what the idea is, and that's passive learning.

Q: In your teaching career have you seen changes in students' abilities to be active learners?

A: Whether they were more active or not in the past, I'm not sure, because we were still more content-centered. That's the way we learned in graduate school. But they did understand the material better and were thus able to ask me questions. Now when I ask if there are any questions and they don't have any, I know it's because they don't understand the idea well enough to ask questions about it. That's the biggest stress I face as a teacher.

Q: What about in your other duties?

A: So much administrative work is required of ordinary faculty members, not just department chairs. For instance, mid-term reports, early warning reports. Unlike when they were in high school, college students should be able to assume responsibility for their own learning. If they're on academic probation, they're supposed to do a work plan with you between semesters. So I think adding those things, plus the fact that we have different challenges now in terms of teaching, create stress. Also, things like assessment. After you teach a course, as you know, Paul, you look back on what seemed most beneficial. The laborious accounting of that is stressful – it's similar to the health care field where nurses spend more time writing charts and writing reports than they do with the patients.

Q: Do you think this comes from people expecting more accountability from the education professions?

A: Yes. And it's not that accountability isn't a good thing – we should be held accountable for what we're doing – but the way of doing it is the way you'd do it in a corporation. Trying to nail down exactly what makes the teaching good and saying how I reached this is really not where learning is. The governance issue also causes stress because more projects are required. There's more demand for people to spend time on things other than teaching. And I think the piece that people don't understand about teaching is that if you don't have reflection time you cannot do quality work in the classroom. If you can't sit down and reflect on the material, process it yourself, and think about how you can communicate this to students, you won't do your job as effectively. It's a catch-22. You're doing all of this to improve quality and be accountable, but in terms of the faculty you're taking them away from the piece that's most important, namely teaching. The same can be said of retention. The faculty's role in retention is quality teaching. And if we're doing all these other things, well the teaching sometimes suffers. Others don't always understand the time commitment that goes into creating good work in the classroom.

Q: How important is the library to your academic well being?

A: Oh, it's absolutely essential. You people provide us with things that would take us a lot more time to produce. You supply us with book reviews, you keep us abreast of new resources. If we were to have to do this, too, we'd have even less time to teach.

Q: In a book titled *The Professors: Who They Are, What They Do*, the author states that 'For some time, the American college professor has been the most pampered professional in our society.' How do you react to that view?

A: I think at big research universities that's probably true. They teach one course, do research, are the prima donnas, have research assistants, etc. In the small college setting I would say that's way off.

Q: When you were in graduate school, thinking about your career, did you consider working at a larger university?

A: I always wanted to teach at a smaller place. My undergraduate work was in Math, and I taught Math and loved it. But when I entered a religious community I was told 'you're going to go on in Philosophy.'

Q: I've heard of that happening to others in religious orders.

A: Yes, they used to do that, but they don't do it now.

Q: Overall, how satisfied are you with your job as it exists today?

A: As it exists today, it's less satisfying. It's these conflicting pulls on you. You hardly have time to accomplish what you want to. People sometimes say 'if only we didn't have students we could get our work done!' There's something wrong when you hear things like that. The satisfying thing about teaching is seeing the students come to appreciate – they don't have to like it – something, to see that light go on and have them think 'yes, that makes sense.' Satisfaction is not getting administrative reports done on time. It's not as much fun as it used to be.

Q: Can you describe your academic career after you graduated from college?

A: When I graduated from high school, I went to Cortland State Teachers College to become a Physical Education teacher. Well, I injured my knee, so they said 'you can go into education.' I wasn't that interested in teaching at that time. I was more interested in pharmacy, but I went into a religious community, the Sisters of St. Joseph of Carondelet, only to learn that they were primarily geared towards producing educators. When I entered them I thought maybe I'd be a missionary at some clinic.

Q: Did you get your credentials from the Teachers College?

A: No, I graduated from the College of St. Rose as a math major. So I started teaching math in junior high school. Then, the order needed someone in Philosophy so I was sent to DePaul University in Chicago. So, they prepared me to teach philosophy at the college level.

Q: So, you received your Masters at DePaul?

A: Yes, but I'm an 'ABD.'

Q: I'm sorry. What does that stand for?

A: 'All but the dissertation.' I had two chapters of the dissertation approved and finished, and then I came here. To have gone through comps and everything, I guess it was kind of foolish not to finish, but even then ... well, most people can't even begin to talk about their PhD research in most of their classes, so for me it didn't make that much of a difference. Much of what you do in graduate school is not directed towards what you're going to be doing as a college faculty member, so you're engaged in things that aren't going to be necessary.

Q: The emphasis is on research, and then when you come to a small institution, the emphasis is on teaching.

A: Yes.

Q: Often, since it's so hard to evaluate teaching, they end up using scholarship as an evaluation tool, since it's easier to – quantitatively at least – evaluate in some ways.

A: And that's another change for our institution. When I first came here, the primary methods of evaluation were academic citizenship and teaching. That's one reason I never finished the dissertation. Fewer people here were doing scholarship – as far as publishing goes anyway – then.

Q: Comment on this statement: since it's so easy to request books via OhioLINK Interlibrary Loan, I now request fewer materials for addition to our local collection.

A: That's true for me. And I depend on Ron [Ron White, another faculty member in Philosophy] to develop the local collection with you.

Q: Can you describe some positive and negative experiences with librarians?

A: The positive experiences I've had with librarians are simply that they were helpful. If you needed anything, if you needed to know exactly what the best periodical would be for a certain topic, they would provide that information. That was true at DePaul and it's been true here. I haven't had any negative experiences, though I haven't had as much experience interacting with librarians because I haven't done as much research as others here have.

Q: What are some common misconceptions that non-academics have about academics?

A: That it's a cushy job. They say 'oh, you only teach four courses, you only work 12 hours a week? And you have the summer off too!' I'm on a nine-month contract, but I'm here every day, even in the summer.

Q: How important is collaboration with librarians in helping your students learn research skills?

A: It's essential because we're not as up on all the online possibilities as you are. And there are lots of things you do that are essential, such as helping us track down students who plagiarize. And the intellectual richness that we experience talking to all of you too.

Q: Who do you think should have the primary responsibility in selecting books and other materials for the college library – faculty, librarians, or a combination of both?

A: I think a combination. Often you've done more research on a book. For example, you can say 'yes, but have you looked at this other title?' that is in a similar field. I've always found the Choice Reviews very helpful because they identify the proper audience for a book – graduate, undergraduate, or faculty. It needs to be a combination. Books and acquisitions – that's your profession. Too often people don't see librarianship as a profession.

Annette Muckerheide, SC, Chair, Biology Department

Q: Can you walk me through your formal education after you received your undergraduate degree?

A: I graduated from this institution in 1963, after which I had a laboratory job for several months, and then I entered the Sisters of Charity in September. I came back to the College and they tried to find a few college courses for me to take – in anything but science! So I took things like Latin American History and Modern Drama. I was a novice in the Sisters of Charity, then I went out teaching in high school. So I didn't begin my Master's until 1969, and I did it on an NSF grant in Iowa, at Drake University, for five summers. I only took the classes on breaks from my teaching. It was a Master's in Science, not Education, but it was geared towards teachers, and it was very general biology. I took everything from Microbiology to Genetics to Field Taxonomy, Embryology, Physiology, and Ecology. A year after I finished that I came to the Mount for a year, taking the place of a faculty member who was on sabbatical. She twisted my arm. I came fully expecting it to last only the one year, but I fell in love with the job. I felt so unprepared, though, that I went back to get my PhD. It took me four years to finish the PhD, going full-time at the University of Cincinnati Medical School. One of the faculty members here at the College held on to the Biology job until I was finished with the doctoral degree. She kept it open for me. When I came back, I think a Post Office custodian was making more money than I was offered. I had the freedom to take the job because I was a Sister of Charity. The Congregation let me do it. I still live on probably less than a Post Office custodian makes and the rest goes to the Motherhouse to support our retired sisters. We have always lived simply.

Q: What are the major sources of stress in your job?

A: [Laughter.] I don't have enough time. There are constant interruptions. I can't get anything done here. It's a lack of time to really think. It's too much to do in too little time. I'm teaching a full load of classes – 12 credits, sometimes 15 – and I'm the chair on top of all of that. Then, we're expected to do scholarship and there are the committees, the endless committees. Being a department chair is middle management. I've got the administration on one hand, faculty on the other. And then I've got the students. I end up advising the hard ones. In other words, the people who come here as transfers, who change majors because they're failing in one major, or the people who have asked for a different adviser.

Q: Why did you decide that you were willing to be chair?

A: I was asked to take over another department when its chair quit, but I didn't want to do it. I made a deal with the Dean that if my then-current chair accepted that job, then I would become the Biology Department's chair. I was originally made chair in 1979, after I'd been back here only one year.

Q: They had a lot of faith in you, didn't they?

A: They know that I'm stubborn, that I'll work all night to get the job done if I have to. After six years of that I took sabbatical leave. When I left on Sabbatical another member of the department said he'd take the Biology chair position. He was still chair when the Dean needed someone to take over the department whose Chair had quit and I moved back into the position.

Q: How important is the library to your academic well-being?

A: It's important. I'm using more and more Internet and electronic resources because of the nature of my discipline. It's here and now. I'm especially appreciative of the electronic resources and of interlibrary loan. I use journals far, far more than books. I love libraries. I love books, but it's getting very hard to get students to read. It breaks my heart when I think of all the knowledge in those covers. I'll never get to it all, but think of all that knowledge!

Q: Can you compare today's students to those you had in the 1970s?

A: They don't read, they can't read, and they won't read. I don't know what it is. They have no use for a newspaper. I'll send them over to the library to find something about microbiology in popular press sources like *Time,* or *The New York Times.* What do they do? They go online to science.com. I guess that's okay, because they did the assignment, but I want them to have the chance to run into something else that interests them.

Q: The serendipity of finding other information while browsing?

A: Yes, just flipping through and finding something else. It doesn't even have to be science-related.

Q: What do you hear about the library from your students?

A: I don't hear much, positive or negative, from students about the library. If there is any negativity, it's a projection of their own feelings of inadequacy. 'The library didn't have it,' they might say. What that really means is that they were too ashamed or shy to ask for help.

Q: What do you think are some common misconceptions that people have about faculty?

A: That we sit in ivory towers, teach our classes, and that's it. We have summers off. And we don't have to study. We know it all already.

Q: In a book titled *The Professors: Who They Are, What They Do,* the author, Herbert Livesey, states 'For some time, the American college professor has been the most pampered professional in our society.' What's your reaction to that statement?

A: Oh, yes, you see that all the time in letters to the editor in newspapers. Pampered? I don't think so. Some might come in, teach their classes, and go home. But they do a lot of work from their home offices, because you don't have a million interruptions there. I don't think most people understand a professor's job. I can't tell you how many times in the last month [July] I've heard, 'oh, you're out now, aren't you?'

Q: I think Livesey feels tenure is a big part of it.

A: I have problems with the whole tenure thing. When I was ready for tenure – and I knew there was no doubt that I'd get it, since I'd been burning the candle at both ends, doing postdoc research at UC [University of Cincinnati] for eleven years while I was teaching here – it was right then that they initiated the rolling contract option. I wrote a letter at the beginning of my tenure portfolio that even though I knew I had to apply for tenure, I would prefer a rolling contract. They gave me tenure. Now we have post-tenure review, so in some sense we're back to rolling contract. Tenure was put in to guarantee academic freedom, and I'm not sure if that's a big issue anymore.

Q: Do you think that tenure's an outdated notion then?

A: I do, but I think we have to be really, really careful now that people have had tenure not to take it away from them.

Q: They'd have to be grandfathered in then?

A: Yes. I thought rolling contract was a step in the right direction.

Q: Can you relate any positive or negative experiences you've had with libraries or librarians?

A: When I was an undergraduate it was all very positive. I fell in love with libraries. When I was getting my Master's degree at Drake I spent a lot of time up at Iowa State getting articles there.

Q: So they didn't have interlibrary loan at Drake?

A: Not then. It was easier for me to run up the road fifty miles to Ames. I was at UC when Medline and electronic searching started. I used to hide from my adviser in the library. There were lots of journals there and I could browse. I learned a lot just from browsing the journals. Back then I'd give the search terms I wanted to use to the librarian and he or she would actually execute the search for me.

Q: That's one of the big changes since then. We've empowered the users to do their own searches.

A: Absolutely. Here that has been so valuable. Before you came, I didn't feel the library was really useful. I spent a lot of time over at UC's library and I'd send the students over there too. But when we started to get the electronic capabilities that changed everything.

Q: How different is your real life as a professor from how you imagined it would be when you were in graduate school?

A: The teaching was already in my bones because I'd taught high school. I'll be honest; I do not enjoy the administrative piece. I don't enjoy the middle management piece, but right now that's the need.

Q: How important is collaborating with campus librarians to help your students learn research skills in your field?

A: In Biology, it's moderately important. Most of us have the research skills. You feed us what we need.

Q: Do the students know about all of our wonderful electronic resources?

A: No, they'd go to Google first. We have to prompt them to go to the library. But I definitely think the librarians should have a role in orienting students to the library.

Q: What are some adjectives you think apply to a successful faculty member?

A: Concerned about students. Intellectually curious. Willing to continue to learn. Willing to be wrong. When faculty are arrogant, I think they're insecure. It takes some chutzpa to get up everyday and get in front of 10, 20, 30, 40 faces and feel like you have to be the font of all knowledge. Nobody is and deep down we all know that. Some people come across as being arrogant and may take it out on librarians, secretaries, and other support staff people, because they have this idea in their head that they should know everything. So I would say, one of the qualities for a good faculty member would be humility. You need to know that you don't know everything.

Q: Any final thoughts?

A: We need to sit down and talk to each other. We don't have time, but we need to. Faculty need to talk to faculty outside of the department.

Richard Sparks, Professor of Education

Q: What are the major sources of stress in your job?

A: Deans, department chairs, and students who are here to play rather than study. Those are the three that come to mind. Deans tend to have unrealistic expectations of what their professors do on a day-to-day basis. The goals a Dean or an administrator might have aren't the same as those a faculty member might have. An administrator tends to see a faculty member as one who is here solely to serve the needs of the College. Whereas the faculty member – especially one who does a lot of scholarship – sees his or her role as not only serving the College, but as someone who is a scholar to the external community, whose job it is to write and disseminate research. Too often – and maybe this only occurs at a small college, I've never been at a university – the total focus tends to be on serving the needs of the College.

Q: Have you noticed a change in your students since you began teaching?

A: Yes, a sea change. When I came here the Mount was all female. It was a college primarily for upper-middle-class Catholic girls. The students were by and large very motivated. They were good academically, good intellectually, good behaviorally. That's not true anymore.

Q: Is it safe to say, then, that your job is less satisfying than it used to be?

A: The teaching part of it is, which is probably why I do so much research.

Q: How do you find time to do your research?

A: I have an extraordinary amount of self-discipline and I'm very organized. I guess I'm just the kind of person who says 'this is what I'm going to do, and this is the date by which I'm going to do it.' I work a lot at night. I don't come to campus one day a week, and that day is devoted to writing, or researching, or consulting.

Q: In a typical week, how many hours do you think you work?

A: My guess would be between 55 and 60.

Q: What are some common misconceptions those outside the academy have about academics?

A: Oh, that's easy. I have only one close friend who is an academic. Everyone else is in business. I'll do it by way of an anecdote. My son is an ice hockey player. He started playing when he was five. All the fathers were standing around together, getting to know each other. Dale says 'yeah, I'm a builder,' and Mike says 'I'm an engineer.' They get to me and ask what I do. I say 'I'm a professor.' Dale, who ended up becoming my best friend, says 'Oh, you don't have a job then.' [Laughter.] That's the perception. That we sit around all day and mull things over and have coffee.

Q: Can you walk me through your formal education, starting with graduate school?

A: I graduated with my BA on – let's say – May 15. I started my Master's on June 1. My BA was in Political Science and History, but I worked my way through school by working as the assistant director of a boy's club. That's where I came into contact with the educational piece, and I knew I wanted to start working with kids with reading disabilities. So I went straight into my Master's. I worked full-time at the boy's club at night and went to school in the day. I did that for 14 months, I think. I immediately went into a teaching job with Cincinnati Public Schools for three years.

Q: At what level?

A: Elementary SBH [severely behaviorally disordered], severe hearing handicapped and learning disabilities. Then, I went into a PhD program for three years. My last year, when I was doing my dissertation, I worked here part-time.

Q: How important is it to collaborate with campus librarians to help your students learn research skills in your field?

A: I think that I probably haven't pursued that much – not that I shouldn't, but I haven't. One of the reasons is that education majors dislike the research process intensely. They don't like to do a research project. They do it because they have to, not because they want to. I collaborate with the librarians by asking them to walk them through and show them how to do a literature search. The students who take the research process seriously find that very helpful. I should probably do that a little more intensely. Students don't really appreciate it. They don't appreciate what I can do for them; they don't appreciate what a librarian can do for them. When they do a review of the literature they do as little as they can. It tends not to be terribly productive. I'm still waiting for one who wants to take the process seriously and really wants to dig for all these sources in the library.

Q: You also work as an independent consultant. What inspired you to work as a professor?

A: I do teach well. Walking into a class with 25 students who have different abilities and behaviors isn't something that's difficult for me. I also enjoy telling people what I know and leading them slowly to that knowledge. I enjoy that process. The other thing that attracted me to the professor's life was that it was an opportunity to control your schedule and have some flexibility in your schedule. The other part of it was the opportunity to read.

Q: How has your use of the library changed over the years?

A: You know how it's changed, because I don't have to contact you as much as I used to! I used to have to contact you to walk me through the different places to find what I needed. The other was that I actually come to the library to pick up things, to look up an article. I had to order things from other campuses, or even go up to another campus to get things directly. Now I ask a question from time to time, but everything's online. I can print articles; I can pretty much get anything I want online now.

Q: What is your vision of the academic library of the future?

A: You're probably going to have fewer people actually coming to the facility. You may wind up with fewer actual volumes because most things will be available online. That's a boon for us since we wouldn't have to actually track them down.

Q: Most faculty members say that their students don't use the library enough. If that's true for you also, whose responsibility is it to increase their use of the library?

A: It's the professor's responsibility, but it's also a shared responsibility between the professor and the student. Librarians shouldn't be out on the corner hawking their wares. In my courses I mainly utilize the electronic reserves. For me that's just wonderful. Where the librarian would come in is if a student has trouble in accessing the articles. It's the same way with the research papers. It's my job to teach them what they need to do in order to write their paper, but it's their job to actually come in and do it.

Q: One adjective sometimes used to describe professors is 'arrogant.' How do you react to a statement like that?

A: I suppose some professors can be, but that's no different from any other profession. The flip side is that some students see professors as arrogant just because professors have a lot of knowledge. I'll use an example. As you know I have a writing policy: one point off for every spelling error, one half point off for every egregious grammar error. No exceptions. That policy has been described by many students as arrogant. I tell them simply that my job isn't to accept them where they are, but to elevate them to where they should be.

Q: Do you think too many young Americans go to college?

A: Yes. I read a book years ago by George Gilder called *Wealth and Poverty*. Gilder pointed out that our society was slowly moving towards what he called 'credentialism.' What he means by this term is that you didn't really need a credential to do a certain job, but the culture was moving to the employer wanting you to have that credential. My best example has always been accountants. Why do they need a college degree? You're good with numbers, so you go to a company, take a math test to confirm this, and then they'll train you to do it their way. I want my doctors to have a credential, and I want my lawyer – God forbid I'll ever need one – to have a credential, but an accountant? We're currently taking into college about 65 per cent of all high-school graduates. The assumption is that they belong to college. Many do not, but if they're going to accept them, some colleges see it as their obligation to see that they graduate.

Q: What should aspiring librarians know about working with faculty?

A: They should be technologically savvy. A lot of professors aren't. So be patient with us. Walking us through things step by step is so valuable, like you did with me. Now I can do these things by myself. The other thing is that sometimes we don't know how to ask for what we want. I may have an overarching concept of what I want, but the librarian needs to be able to narrow it down. You know the sources well and I don't. Just because we know something in a particular topic area, it doesn't mean that we know where to look for it or how to find it.

John Trokan, Chair, Religious and Pastoral Studies Department

Q: What are the major sources of stress in your job?

A: In terms of stress it would be trying to balance the different areas of expectations: citizenship, scholarship, and teaching. It's particularly complex since we're a small college, and the faculty have to wear so many hats. Personally, it's trying to balance the administrative piece – recruitment and admission for our graduate program – with trying to carve out the quality time you need to continue to make a contribution, to stay fresh in the field.

Q: How different do you find your job from what you expected it might be like when you were in graduate school?

A: Looking at it when I was younger, I really saw the joy in it, both the teaching interaction with students and the depth of learning I could enjoy. And I think I have actually experienced both. I feel like I'm the luckiest man in the world in terms of being able to get up in the morning and do what I do. The one thing I didn't see when I was young is the administrative piece, and it grows in complexity each year.

Q: How did you feel when you were offered the department chair position? Did you have doubts as to whether or not you wanted it?

A: When that happened we were at a very conflicted time in the history of our department. I felt very affirmed in terms of my administrative skills, and I knew I could serve the college well as far as taking our department in certain directions. When I said yes to it, though, I thought it would be a three-year commitment, and I've been doing it now for ten years! In my own heart I felt that a rotating chair position was healthy for the college, for its mission, and for the individuals involved. But what's played out is that we don't have any other tenured people to be able to take over the department. I have three untenured junior faculty at this point, so it will be a number of years before this changes.

Q: Please walk me through your formal education after you received your undergraduate degree.

A: Let's see if I can recall [laughs]. I did my undergraduate work at Marquette in theology, and then I continued on and did my Masters with no break. Actually, there was a break in finishing the Masters. I did the coursework, but it took me another two years to finish the language exam and write the thesis because I was working part-time during the Masters, and it moved to full-time after I got the coursework done. Plus I had married, and so I was trying to balance and juggle all of that. Then, there was a six-year break between finishing the Master's and starting the doctoral program. I served the Archdiocese of Milwaukee doing ministry formation work – which involved lots of part-time teaching. Teaching was the part of the job I really loved. It took three more years to finish the doctorate in ministry.

Q: How important is collaborating with campus librarians in helping students learn research skills in your field?

A: I've always believed it's essential in terms of the ability to develop their skills as well as their access to current scholarship. It's one of the things I've felt so blessed with here in terms of the quality of the librarians' work and their commitment to excellence and service. Considering the naiveté of our undergraduate students knowing what good sources are and how to find and document them, it's been critical. Our graduate students for the most part are adult learners who might not have been in school for twenty years, so when they come back they need support and shepherding to believe they can use these new tools. It's just been invaluable.

Q: Who should have primary responsibility for developing the library collection: faculty, librarians, or should it be some sort of combination?

A: I believe in partnership, and we've really done that in the time that I've been here. It's great when you or one of your staff finds something and passes it on to me. You've been so responsive to the requests we've had for our collection, it's made it easy.

Q: Do any memories of librarians or libraries stand out for you during your academic career?

A: One of the things I appreciate about the library – in addition to the ability to connect with new ideas – is the peace. It's kind of like walking into a chapel. For me, it's a sacred space. It is special in terms of the opportunity to grow in insight that this space provides. And the solitude.

Q: What are some common misconceptions that people outside of the profession have about the professor's job?

A: Well, I think one of the big misconceptions is that this is a part-time job and that we're off in the summer [laughs]. It's not a 24/7 kind of thing, but it is a 12-month job for me. It is a vocation and teaching is something I do with my whole person. It's a 12-month commitment in terms of nurturing the skills I have and bringing them into every class I teach. I look at it as a covenant. When we sit down in class with the syllabus, we're really partnering in this endeavor. I have to do everything I can to be as knowledgeable to facilitate that learning as I possibly can. Some days I do that well, some days not so well, but the commitment to continue to try to do that is always there.

Q: Given all your other duties, how hard is it to stay up to date in your field and do research?

A: That is probably the most challenging part. It's just very hard when you're chair to be able to do that. I relish the opportunity to go to professional conferences and present papers. I wish I had more time to write. That's taken a back seat to recruitment since I've been chair. If I don't recruit, we don't have a program. That's a lived tension.

Q: Can you think of some words that aptly describe the good professor?

A: Passion, commitment, thirst for new knowledge, and relationship – in terms of what the partnership is in the learning process. Dialog. For me, good theology is always dialogical. It's an activity of the community. It's not just what Karl Rahner or Elizabeth Johnson wrote, but how we reflect our traditions, our experiences, and our culture together as a community. So being able to facilitate that dialog is crucial.

Q: What have you learned from your students?

A: A tremendous amount. I really believe that my students are the ones who have made me a good teacher. I had an experience here early on teaching a lot of Excel students [these are remedial students who often need extra help]. One particular semester I had about six in one section. There was a young woman, Kate, in this section who came in and sat in the first row every day. And from day one her hand would always go up: 'Dr. Trokan, would you explain that?' She had been a car accident victim where another car flew over the median and hit head on the car she was in. The driver in her car was killed and the doctors said she was lucky to have lived through it. She was in a coma as a result of the accident, and when she came out of it she essentially had to relearn everything she'd ever learned: eating, walking, and going to the bathroom. And there she was, sitting in class, wide-eyed. That was my invitation to look at learning from the student's side of the desk and rethink everything I'd been doing. That was a tremendous gift for me, because I rethought how I presented material, and how we discussed it. Students are continuing to change, so that every three to five years I'm having to look very carefully at what I'm doing from a methodological perspective in order to be effective. Today's students are different from those from five years ago. If I go into the classroom with the same expectations I had about the former students, it won't work. So a lot of it is being attentive and learning from the students themselves. What makes the connection for them? What sparks their interest? I think they're my greatest teachers.

Q: Can you talk about the impact of information technology on your teaching?

A: I was lab rat #1 with ISS [Information Services and Systems]. If they could teach me to do it, they could teach anybody. I embrace it because I see it as a marvelous tool in terms of enhancing your work. I've done a lot of PowerPoint authoring and used WebCT quite often, and I enjoy doing that. It really has deepened the learning and made it much more accessible. It can also be utilized in regard to on- and off-campus use. I'm still looking for new ways to change and adapt and use it in the classroom. The only real downside is the distraction piece in regard to classroom use of laptops. You do get the student who wants to do their e-mail, or is online trying to buy a new car rather than focusing in on the new material. We went through this with the cell phone too. I just ask students to respect each other's space. If you're using your laptop inappropriately, others are going to see that, and that's a distraction. That's one downside. The other is that anyone looking for a down and dirty paper is going to want to click and do sloppy stuff. They're not going to do quality work. Some students are still learning these lessons.

Q: What role should the academic library play on the college campus?

A: From my perspective it's a hub, the research center. One of the things that I think you've done very well is opening up the traditional library format to help our campus experience the library as a learning center without boundaries. I appreciate the variety and diversity of activities that you've offered, particularly in the last couple of years. I think it's an ongoing challenge to get students to use the library. It's a community space where marvelous things can happen. People gather and share there.

Q: Any final thoughts?

A: Specifically, the electronic reserves service is just the cat's meow. The ability to put up current things and have them so readily accessible for students is great. Last night we had our last Lakota class and part of the assignment was that they had to research the issue of housing on the reservation. It was just so marvelous to see that a number of students had gone to the electronic reserves and found the articles that were there on housing and were using those insights in their own discussion of the issue. That's what it's all about, learning how to synthesize and integrate that sort of information.

Ron White, Professor, Humanities Department

Q: What are the major sources of stress related to your job?

A: Meetings. College service. That's 99 per cent of it.

Q: When you were in graduate school planning on this career, how different was your vision of the job from the real thing as you've experienced it so far?

A: I didn't understand the requirements for promotion. Most places have something that resembles scholarship, something that resembles teaching, something that resembles service. That's pretty traditional. But here the commitment to service has always been in my mind fairly ambiguous and more time-consuming than I expected. I never thought much about the service component, because all I did in graduate school was teach and write. That's probably just me, though.

Q: That's interesting because many of the people I've talked to have said that scholarship was the hardest part of the job for them.

A: I've done scholarship for thirty years. I do it because I love it. In summer I get up every morning at 5:30, drink a cup of coffee and write until noon. It opens up new inquiries for learning and it makes me a better teacher. I know many of the top scholars in my field. I go to meetings with them. That's not work, that's fun. Teaching for me is fun. If I were a millionaire I'd still teach and do scholarship. Forcing people to spend time in meetings and doing things that never add up to anything, wasting time – that's work.

Q: Can you talk about some positive and negative experiences you've had with libraries or librarians?

A: I think you've been the first librarian that I've really gotten to know. I've always been pretty good at finding my way around the library, doing a lot of my own stuff. I've always asked questions when I've needed to. I can't say that I've had any negative experiences.

Q: How have libraries changed since you first started using them?

A: It's the electronic media. Going from cards, a manual system, to the electronic library. Since I've been here I've seen the changes, how we gradually went from paper to electronics here. That's been the biggest change, that and being able to get materials so easily from other libraries through OhioLINK. They had similar things in the state of Kentucky, but they had such a huge library that I didn't need to use the service.

Q: Since it's so easy to request things from OhioLINK, is it fair to say that you're less concerned about developing our local collection?

A: Yes and no. I think there are some books that we really should have. You can't count on students to use interlibrary loan because they're not good planners. For them to plan to use OhioLINK, they'd have to get their research going earlier. I'd like to see both. Then the question is, which books? Who decides that is another question.

Q: Since we're on that topic, who should have the primary responsibility for developing the local collection, the faculty, librarians, or some sort of combination?

A: Probably a combination. I've been here under all three systems. It used to be that we would find books on our own and forward them to the library to be ordered. There are times when I'd be good at it and times when I wouldn't. Me being the one responsible for looking for books, that's just one more responsibility that takes me away from my research. I think that's being a little bit idealistic, depending just on the faculty.

Q: With all your other duties it can be hard to find the time.

A: Yes, it's hard to find a strategic time to do it. I bump into books all the time and think 'that would be a good one for our library.' But to get from that thought to actually recommending it formally, that's a whole other thing.

Q: I know that you've done a lot of reviews for *Choice*. What in your mind makes a good book review?

A: *Choice* is a model. They have nice, short book reviews by people who know what they're doing. What they ask me to do is basically give a quick summary of what the book's about, plug it into some larger issue that it addresses, and then try to find if there are other books similar to it, and if so to give references to them. To find out what area, what genre of philosophy they fit in. I do a lot of things on social and political philosophy and western liberalism. Teachers often are looking for books that cover one specific area.

Q: And they ask you to include what level of readership it's intended for, right?

A: I'll make that determination, whether it's general public, upper division, lower division undergraduate, graduate, or faculty. I've had a handful of graduate books, but most of them are for undergraduates. I ask myself, 'would my students be able to deal with this?' I look for that in the reviews I read, because *Choice* caters to small colleges. Most of the books I see are relevant to undergraduates, but that doesn't mean I recommend them all the time. I've panned a few. I've gotten nasty letters from authors on occasions.

Q: Take me through your formal education, starting with your graduate school days.

A: I graduated from Eastern Kentucky University with a double major of art and philosophy. Then, I went to graduate school at the University of Kentucky. I had some connections there and I got a teaching assistantship. I was there for two full years. I finished my Master's thesis and lost it! But I didn't need it. I got accepted at Michigan State for a PhD in philosophy. I had some personal complications and ended up in debt and had to drop out and come back to this area of the country. I spent a couple of years working and started teaching part time. I got into a History of Science program at the University of Kentucky, and that's where I ended up getting my doctoral degree.

Q: I haven't spoken with many people who have just followed all the steps without some sort of interruption.

A: I changed completely. I had to learn everything in history all over again. My Master's didn't count. I started right from scratch. I went right through at that stage. I wrote my dissertation in a year. I was pretty efficient. I had that lay off, but what a lot of people don't realize is that in graduate school two hard things you have to deal with are money and relationships. There's a lot of stress on you at that time.

Q: What sort of changes have you noticed in students through the years?

A: I taught as an adjunct at the University of Kentucky for three years while I was looking for a full-time job. There was a lot of variety in the students. Out of a class of thirty students, I'd have five or six who could have been at Harvard, and I'd have another five or six who didn't belong in college at all.

Q: How do you teach to a class like that?

A: You just do the best you can. I always try to teach what I'm interested in, because if I try to teach something watered down, I lose interest in it, and the students pick up on that. I've always kept good relationships with students so that they could come and see me. I've always made a lot of student friends. That's the secret, to be approachable. Frankly, though, the people at the bottom are not the ones who come to see me. The ones who come to see me have always been at the top of the class. In fact, every year I tell students that if they need help in writing essays to come by and see me, and I'd say nine out of ten students who come see me would have gotten As anyway. The people at the bottom won't come to see me and they complain in the end that they didn't get a very good grade. That's one of the real puzzles I haven't been able to crack yet. Lots of time they're the ones who are working and have lots of other things going on. They come to their classes, then run out to go to work. Back to your other question, that's a big difference I see now. When I was at school I never knew students who worked. Everybody went to school full time. And that influences what you can do in class, of course. Out of a class of thirty I'd say you're lucky if you get ten who have read the assignment. It's just a reality. I make my lectures available on the Web; I make PowerPoint slides for my lectures so that they can pull those things up. I make it easier for them so that they can get some content other than just what I say.

Q: You're happy incorporating technology into the classroom then?

A: Yes. The way I do it, it's helped. The least useful thing is really the laptops in the classroom. I've been in other people's classrooms observing teaching, and I sit in the back and look around the room. Seventy-five per cent of the students are doing instant messaging or something and others are on websites. It's a distraction. I wish the students would use the laptops the way I want them to, but I can't say that they really do.

Q: How important is the library to the academic well-being of the college, or to your academic well-being?

A: I think it's important, but given the way students are now, it's harder and harder to send them to the library to do research. It's hard to require them to come to the library and do a research project the way we might have years ago. I don't require a research paper any longer. They really don't spend the time doing the necessary research. They won't take the time to do interlibrary loan. I give them take-home essay exams, five pages long, usually three to a course. I ask questions that are weird enough that it's hard for them to find much of them on the Web. I'd never ask them to do a term paper on Machiavelli because half of them would just use something off the Web.

Q: I know you bring your students into the library for one of your courses.

A: Yes, that's PHI 240. They have to do a panel discussion. I send them over in groups of three and ask them to research their position. For example, if they're doing something on world hunger, I'll have one of them look at developmentalism, Peter Singer, or the Catholic Church. Someone else might research Malthusianism, and someone else representing libertarianism and different points of view on that. I'll have them research those specific topics and I'll tell them specifically what to look for. I'll walk around and help them find what they need. I pretty much know where the books are in the library. I show them the indexes and some of the other things that will be helpful to them. That's the only class I do that for. It's not really making them write a research paper, it's making sure that they know enough about their topic to be able to do their panel discussion.

Q: Complete this sentence. I wish our campus library ...

A: I'd like to say, 'had more books,' because I don't think the students use OhioLINK often enough for that to be any kind of substitute. I know the faculty use it, but I wonder how many undergraduates use it.

Q: The numbers have been going up.

A: That's good. I'd say our electronic holdings are as good as anybody's. That's all state of the art. People at the desk are always helpful.

Q: So developing the core collection would be most important in your eyes?

A: Yes, but I'm not sure how we'd go about that. I'm not sure I'd know what books to buy in philosophy that people would access on a regular basis. I'm reading a book right now by Peter Singer called *The President of Good and Evil: The Ethics of George Bush*. It's awesome. I don't think I could use it in my classes because it's too political, though. Singer's the most famous and influential philosopher in the world right now.

References

Adams, H. (1988) *Academic Tribes*. Urbana: University of Illinois Press.

Allen, B. and Hirshon, A. (1998) 'Hanging together to avoid hanging separately: opportunities for academic libraries and consortia,' *Information Technology and Libraries*, 17 (1): 36–44.

Almanac Issue 2004–05 (2004) *Chronicle of Higher Education*.

American Library Association (2003) *The Campaign for America's Libraries @ Your Library. Toolkit for Academic and Research Libraries*. Chicago: ALA.

Arp, L. (1990) 'Information literacy or bibliographic instruction: semantics or philosophy?' *RQ*, 30: 46–9.

Alkins, P. (1996) 'On chairing a campus committee: leadership at Hope College,' *College and Research Libraries News*, 57 (10): 652, 654.

Auer, N.J., Seamans, N.H. and Pelletier, L. (2003) 'Peer advising in the research process: a year of student success,' in J. Nims and E. Owens (eds), *Managing Library Instruction Programs in Academic Libraries*. Ann Arbor, MI: Pierian Press, pp. 25–30.

Biggs, M. (1981) 'Sources of tension and conflict between librarians and faculty,' *Journal of Higher Education*, 52 (2): 182–201.

Bingham, R. (1979) 'Collection development in university libraries: an investigation of the relationship between categories of selectors and usage of selected items.' Unpublished doctoral dissertation, Rutgers University.

Boice, R. (2000) *Advice for New Faculty Members: Nihil Nimus*. Boston: Allyn & Bacon.

Bowen, H. (1986) *American Professors: A National Resource Imperiled*. New York: Oxford University Press.

Brandtz, M. (2002) 'Library-sponsored faculty book-buying trips,' *College and Research Libraries News*, 63 (4): 264–6, 292.

Breivik, P. and McDermand, R. (2004) 'Campus partnerships building on success,' *College and Research Libraries News*, 65 (4): 210–12, 215.

Budd, J. and Adams, K. (1989) 'Allocation formulas in practice,' *Library Acquisitions: Practice and Theory*, 13: 381–90.

Buis, E. (1993) 'Let's make sure we are not part of the problem: a librarian's lament,' *Collection Building*, 13 (1): 21–3.

Burkhardt, J.M., MacDonald, M.C., and Rathemacher, A.J. (2003) *Teaching Information Literacy*. Chicago: ALA.

Cain, M.E. (2002) 'The freedom of "Yes" – a personal view of service,' *Educause Quarterly*, 3: 7–10.

Cardwell, C. (2001) 'Faculty: an essential resource for reference librarians,' *Reference Librarian*, 73: 253–63.

Carpenter, E. (1997) 'Purchasing monographs in view of OhioLINK.' Unpublished manuscript.

Carter, M. (1974) *Building Library Collections*. Metuchen, NJ: Scarecrow Press.

Cawthorne, J. (2003) 'Integrating outreach and building partnerships: expanding our role in the learning community,' *College and Research Libraries News*, 64 (10): 666–9, 681.

Chu, F.T. (1997) 'Librarian–faculty relations in collection development,' *Journal of Academic Librarianship*, 23: 15–20.

Connell, T.H. (1991) 'Comparing the circulation of library materials ordered by faculty and librarians,' *Collection Management*, 14 (1–2): 73–84.

Cooper, C. and Gardner, B. (2001) 'Coming full circle: a library's adventure in collaboration,' *Kentucky Libraries*, 65 (3): 23–5.

Crawford, W. (2003) 'Libraries, e-books, and monolithic solutions,' *American Libraries*, 34 (4): 88.

Cunningham, T.H. and Lanning, S. (2002) 'New frontier trail guides: faculty–librarian collaboration on information literacy,' *Reference Services Review*, 30(4): 343–8.

Davis, P. (1997) 'What computer skills do employers expect from recent college graduates?' *T.H.E. Journal*, 25(2): 74–8.

Davis, P. (1999) 'How undergraduates learn computer skills: results of a survey and focus group,' *T.H.E. Journal*, 26(9): 68–71.

Dickinson, D. (1981) 'A rationalist's critique of book selection for academic libraries,' *Journal of Academic Librarianship*, 7: 138–43.

Dorner, J. (2003) 'Information literacy assessment tool,' in E.F. Avery (ed.), *Assessing Student Learning Outcomes for Information Literacy Instruction in Academic Institutions*. Chicago: ALA, pp. 103–7.

Dukes, R.J. (1983) 'Faculty/library relations in acquisitions and collection development: the faculty perspective,' *Library Acquisitions*, 3: 221–4.

Engel, D. and Antell, K. (2004) 'The life of the mind: a study of faculty spaces in academic libraries,' *College and Research Libraries*, 65 (1): 8–26.

Evans, G. (1970) 'Book selection and book collection usage in academic libraries,' *Library Quarterly*, 40: 297–308.

Falk, G. (1990) *The Life of the Academic Professional in America: An Inventory of Tasks, Tensions, and Achievements*. Lewiston, NY: E. Mellen Press.

Farber, E. (1974) *The Academic Library: Essays in Honor of Guy R. Lyle*. Metuchen, NJ: Scarecrow Press.

Farber, E. (1992) 'Teachers as learners – the application of BI,' in L. Shirato (ed.), *Working with Faculty in the New Electronic Library*. Ann Arbor, MI: Pierian Press, pp. 1–5.

Farber, E. (1995) 'Plus ça change …,' *Library Trends*, 44 (2): 430–8.

Farber, E. (1999) 'Faculty–librarian cooperation: a personal retrospective,' *Reference Services Review*, 27 (3): 229–34.

Finnegan, D. (1996) *Faculty and Faculty Issues in Colleges and Universities*. Needham Heights, MA: Simon & Schuster Custom Publications.

Fonfa, R. (1998) 'From faculty to librarian materials selection: an element in the professionalization of librarianship,' in T.F. Mech and G.B. McCabe (eds), *Leadership and Academic Librarians*. Westport, CT: Greenwood Press, pp. 22–38.

Freedman, M. (1979) *Academic Culture and Faculty Development*. Berkeley, CA: Montaigne Press.

Gabelnick, F., MacGregor, J., Matthews, S., and Smith, B. (1990) *Learning Communities: Creating Connections among Students, Faculty and Disciplines*. San Francisco: Jossey-Bass.

Gaines, A.J. (1994) 'Farmington plan,' in W.A. Wiegand and D.G. Davis (eds), *Encyclopedia of Library History*. New York: Garland, p. 193.

Gardner, C.A. (1985) 'Book selection policies in the college library: a reappraisal,' *College and Research Libraries*, 46: 140–6.

German, L. and Schmidt, K. (2001) 'Honoring faculty: book plates to celebrate faculty achievements,' *College and Research Libraries News*, 62 (11): 1066–7, 1130.

Geyer, J.E. (1977) *A Comparative Analysis of Book Selection Agents and Tools with Student Use at the Long Beach Community College Library*. EdD Dissertation, University of Southern California.

Gordon, I. (2000) 'Asserting our collection development roles,' *College and Research Libraries News*, 61 (8): 687–9.

Gore, D. (1966) 'The mismanagement of college libraries: a view from the inside,' *AAUP Bulletin*, 52: 46–51.

Gore, D. (1982) 'Something there is that doesn't love a professor,' *Library Journal*, 107: 686–91.

Hardesty, L. (1986) 'Book selection for undergraduate libraries: a study of faculty attitudes,' *Journal of Academic Librarianship*, 12 (1): 19–25.

Hardesty, L. (1988) 'Use of library materials at a small liberal arts college: a replication,' *Collection Management*, 10 (3/4): 61–80.

Hardesty, L. (1991) *Faculty and the Library: The Undergraduate Experience*. Norwood, NJ: Ablex.

Hardesty, L. (1995) 'Faculty culture and bibliographic instruction: an exploratory analysis,' *Library Trends*, 44 (2): 339–67.

Hardesty, L. (1999) 'Reflections on 25 years of library instruction: have we made progress?' *Reference Services Review*, 27 (3): 242–6.

Hawes, G. and Hawes, L. (eds.) (1982) *The Concise Dictionary of Education*. New York: Van Nostrand Reinhold.

Herring, M. (2001) '10 reasons why the internet is no substitute for a library,' *American Libraries*, 32 (4): 76–8.

Holley, E.G. (1985) 'Defining the academic librarian,' *College and Research Libraries*, 46: 462–8.

Holtze, T. (2002) *100 Ways to Reach Your Faculty*. Presented at the annual meeting of the American Librarian Association, Atlanta, GA.

Hostetler, K. (2001) *The Art and Politics of College Teaching: A Practical Guide for the Beginning Professor*. New York: P. Lang.

Howe, N. and Strauss, W. (2000) *Millennials Rising: The Next Great Generation*. New York: Vintage Books.

Isaacson, D. (2001) 'Librarians who lunch,' *College and Research Libraries News*, 62 (5): 532–3.

Jenkins, P. (1996) 'Faculty priorities: where does material selection stand?' *Collection Building*, 15 (1): 19–20.

Jenkins, P. (1999) 'Book reviews and faculty book selection,' *Collection Building*, 18 (1): 4–5.

Jenkins, P. (2003) 'The approval plan: what's in it for small OhioLINK libraries?' *Library Collections, Acquisitions, and Technical Services*, 27: 179–81.

Jenkins, P. (2004) 'SWORCS: a work in process,' *Against the Grain*, 16 (3): 30–4.

Julien, H. and Given, M. (2002) 'Faculty–librarian relationships in the information literacy context: a content analysis of librarians' expressed attitudes and experiences,' *Canadian Journal of Information and Library Science*, 27 (3): 65–87.

Kempcke, K. (2002) 'The art of war for librarians: academic culture, curriculum reform, and wisdom from Sun Tzu,' *Portal*, 2 (4): 529–51.

Kuo, H. (2000) 'Surveying faculty book selection in a comprehensive university library,' *Collection Building*, 19 (1): 27–35.

Larson, C.M. (1998) 'What I want in a faculty member: a reference librarian's perspective,' *Reference and User Services Quarterly*, 259–61.

Levine, A. (1978) *Handbook on Undergraduate Curriculum*. San Francisco: Jossey-Bass.

Lindholm, J. et al. (2002) *The American College Teacher: National Norms for the 2001–2002 HERI Faculty Survey*. Los Angeles: Higher Education Research Institute.

Lindsay, E. (2000) 'Undergraduate students as peer instructors: one way to expand library instruction and reference services,' *LOEX News*, 27 (4): 7ff.

Lippincott, J. (2002) 'Developing collaborative relationships: librarians, students, and faculty creating learning communities,' *College and Research Libraries News*, 63 (3): 190–2.

Livesey, H. (1975) *The Professors: Who They Are, What They Do, What They Really Want and What They Need*. New York: Charterhouse.

Malone, D. and Videon, C. (2003) *First Year Student Library Instruction Programs*, CLIP Notes #33. Chicago: ACRL.

Mason, M. and Goulden, M. (2002) 'Do babies matter? The effect of family formation on the lifelong careers of academic men and women,' *Academe*, 88 (6): 21–7.

McCabe, G. (1989) *Operations Handbook for the Small Academic Library*. New York: Greenwood Press.

McKinzie, S. (1997) 'Librarians and faculty in tandem: taking our cues from the evening news,' *Reference and User Services Quarterly*, 37 (1): 19–21.

Mech, T. and McCabe, G. (1998) *Leadership and Academic Librarians*. Westport, CT: Greenwood Press.

Melko, M. (1998) *A Professor's Work*. Lanham, MD: University Press of America.

Menges, R. (1999) *Faculty in New Jobs: A Guide to Settling In, Becoming Established, and Building Institutional Support.* San Francisco: Jossey-Bass.

Moore, M. and Kearsley, G. (1996) *Distance Education: A Systems View.* Belmont, CA: Wadsworth.

National Labor Relations Board v. *Yeshiva University* (1979) 444 US 672.

Neville, R., Hunt, C.C., and Williams, J. (1998) 'Faculty–library teamwork in book ordering,' *College and Research Libraries*, 59 (6): 524–33.

Niles, N. (2001) 'The end of BI: will classroom faculty replace us in the new millennium?' in J.K. Nims and A. Andrew (eds), *Library User Education in the New Millennium: Blending Traditions, Trends, and Innovation.* Ann Arbor, MI: Pierian Press, pp. 97–100.

Nims, J. and Owens, E. (2003) *Managing Library Instruction Programs in Academic Libraries.* Ann Arbor, MI: Pierian Press.

Nowakowski, F.C. (1993) 'Faculty support information literacy,' *College and Research Libraries News*, 3: 124.

Primary Research Group Inc. (2003) *Training College Students in Information Literacy.* New York: Primary Research Group Inc.

Ragains, P. (2001) 'A primer on developing and using course-related library web pages,' *Research Strategies*, 18 (1): 85–93.

Raspa, D. and Ward, D. (2000) *The Collaborative Imperative: Librarians and Faculty Working Together in the Information Universe.* Chicago: ACRL.

Reichel, M. (2001) 'ACRL: the learning community for excellence in academic libraries,' *College and Research Libraries News*, 62 (8): 818–21.

Ricigliano, L. (2001) 'After X Comes Y: teaching the next generation,' in J.K. Nims and A. Andrew (eds), *Library User Education in the New Millennium: Blending Traditions, Trends, and Innovation.* Ann Arbor, MI: Pierian Press, pp. 121–9.

Riedel, T. (2003) 'Added value, multiple choices: librarian/faculty collaboration in online course development,' *Journal of Library Administration*, 37 (3/4): 477–87.

Ryland, J. (1982) 'Collection development and selection: who should do it?' *Library Acquisitions: Practice and Theory*, 6 (1): 13–7.

Sample content (2004) 'Lesson 2: An historical overview of service.' Available at: *http://courses.worldcampus.psu.edu/welcome/hrim315/x02pw/samplecontent.shtml* (retrieved 19 October 2004).

Sandler, M.S. (1984) 'Organizing effective faculty participation in collection development,' *Collection Management*, 6: 63–73.

Schad, J. (1987) 'Fairness in book fund allocation,' *College and Research Libraries*, 48: 479–86.

Schappert, D.G. (1989) 'Allocation formulas: the core of the acquisitions process,' in G.B. McCabe (ed.), *Operations Handbook for the Small Academic Library*. New York: Greenwood Press, pp. 137–44.

Scherdin, M.J. (2002) 'How well do we fit? Librarians and faculty in the academic setting,' *Portal*, 2 (2): 237–53.

Sellen, M. (1985) 'Book selection in the college library: the faculty perspective,' *Collection Building*, 7 (1): 4–10.

Shapiro, J.J. and Hughes, S.K. (1996) 'Information literacy as a liberal art,' *Educom Review*, 31 (2). Available at: *http://www.educause.edu/pub/er/review/reviewArticles/31231.html* (retrieved 29 August 2004).

Smiley, J. (1995) *Moo*. New York: Knopf.

Smith, R.L. (1997) 'Philosophical shift: teach the faculty to teach information literacy.' Available at: *http://www.ala.org/ala/acrlbucket/nashville1997pap/smith.htm* (retrieved 27 October 2004).

Sonntag, G. (2001) 'Report on the national information literacy survey,' *College and Research Libraries News*, 62 (10): 996–1001.

Stahl, A. (1997) 'What I want in a librarian,' *Reference and User Services Quarterly*, 37 (2): 133–5.

Stebelman, S., Siggins, J., Nutty, D., and Long, C. (1999) 'Improving library relations with the faculty and university administrators: the role of the faculty outreach librarian,' *College and Research Libraries*, 60 (2): 121–30.

Thompson, C. and Smith, B. (1992) 'Are college graduates missing the corporate boat?' *HR Focus*, 69 (4): 23.

Toft, Z. (2004) 'What can librarians do for us? An academic's perspective,' *Library and Information Update*, 3 (1): 42–3.

Trinchera, T. (2000) 'Faculty: the hidden problem patron,' *The U*N*A*B*A*S*H*E*D Librarian*, 116: 19–22.

Tuten, J.H. (1995) *Allocation Formulas in Academic Libraries*, CLIP Note #22. Chicago: ACRL.

Vidor, D.L. and Futas, E. (1988) 'Effective collection developers: librarians or faculty?' *Library Resources and Technical Services*, 32: 127–36.

Vocational Training News (2003) 'Teens say tech knowledge increases potential jobs,' 34 (12): 6.

Westbrook, L. and Tucker, S. (2002) 'Understanding faculty information needs,' *Reference and User Services Quarterly*, 42 (2): 144–8.

Wiegand, W. (2005) 'Critiquing the curriculum,' *American Libraries*, 36 (1): 58–61.

Williams, D. (1998) 'The library director as a campus leader,' in T.F. Mech and G.B. McCabe (eds), *Leadership and Academic Librarians*. Westport, CT: Greenwood Press, pp. 39–54.

Wilson, L. (1995) *The Academic Man: A Study in the Sociology of a Profession*. New Brunswick, NJ: Transaction.

Wilson, L.A. (1995) 'Instruction as a reference service,' in R.E. Bopp and L.C. Smith (eds), *Reference and Information Services: An Introduction*. Englewood, CO: Libraries Unlimited, pp. 152–84.

Woodsworth, A. (1998) 'Faculty: the minefields of the library,' *Library Journal*, 123 (9): 54.

Yang, Z. (2000) 'University faculty's perception of a library liaison program: a case study,' *Journal of Academic Librarianship*, 26 (2): 124–8.

Index

Printed in the United States
71171LV00002B/272

9 781843 341161